SURVIVING COLUMBINE

SURVIVING COLUMBINE

HOW FAITH HELPS US FIND PEACE WHEN TRAGEDY STRIKES

Edited by
LIZ CARLSTON

Contributors
LIZ CARLSTON
AMBER HUNTINGTON
MICHAEL JOHNSON
KATHY JOHNSON

Illustrations by
KATHY CARLSTON

DESERET
BOOK

SALT LAKE CITY, UTAH

Text © 2004 Elizabeth E. Carlston

Illustrations © 2004 Kathrine M. Carlston

Visit us at deseretbook.com

Library of Congress Cataloging-in-Publication Data

Carlston, Liz.
  Surviving Columbine : how faith helps us find peace when tragedy strikes / Liz Carlston.
       p.   cm.
  ISBN 1-59038-266-8 (pbk.)
    1. School shootings—Colorado—Littleton.   2. Columbine High School (Littleton, Colo.)—Students—Biography.   3. Christian teenagers—Colorado—Littleton—Biography.   I. Title.
  LB3013.33.C6C37 2004
  277.3'0829'0922—dc22   2003024999

Printed in the United States of America   54459-028P
Malloy Lithographing Incorporated, Ann Arbor, MI

10   9   8   7   6   5   4   3   2   1

DEDICATION

In loving memory of the good they stood for—five people who are loved. Because of their choices, they made a difference:

William "Dave" Sanders
October 22, 1951–April 20, 1999
Teacher and Coach at Columbine High School

Theresa Lara Miller
August 11, 1958–December 2, 2002
Teacher at Columbine High School

Linda Carpenter Madsen
March 8, 1943–April 21, 1999
Friend

Elizabeth Ann Cramer Brown
March 29, 1959–August 10, 1987
Aunt and Sister-in-law

Adah Culler Morgan
October 9, 1921–July 16, 2001
"Grandma Adah"

And special thanks to Elaine Fox Huntington
"Grandma Elaine"
Thank you for your kindness and
support during a difficult time.

EPIGRAPH

"Next to the bestowal of life itself, the right to direct that life is God's greatest gift to man. Agency is the impelling source of the soul's progress. It is the purpose of the Lord that man become like Him. In order for man to achieve this, it was necessary for the creator first to make him free."

—David O. McKay

CONTENTS

ILLUSTRATIONS

ACKNOWLEDGMENTS

Thank you to Sandra Phillips for your mentoring, constant encouragement, and advice. Truly, I am a more confident and able person because of your support and love. Thank you to Colleen Whitley at the BYU Publishing Lab, who helped get this manuscript to the right people. Thanks also to Gabrielle Harris, who contributed to the text. Thanks to my sister Kathy Carlston, who created the illustrations found in these pages as part of her grief therapy and graciously allowed me to use them in this book. And a very special thanks to my mom, Eileen Sorensen Carlston, Ed.D., for editing assistance.

Most of all, I hope this book will stand as a tribute to those individuals who made good choices that made a difference in so many lives. This book is a testament of the existence of Jesus Christ as well as of his healing hand and his unending love for all of us. I hope this book will give those who read it a sense of both the positive and negative consequences of our choices. May we all choose to take the road of optimism, patience, and desire to make lives better.

PREFACE

A little after 11:00 A.M. on Tuesday, April 20, 1999, two senior boys at Columbine High School parked their cars and made final preparations for their carefully planned assault with guns and bombs on the school community. They shot their first victims at 11:19 A.M.; their last shots were fired by 12:08 P.M., when they took their own lives in the school library. They murdered twelve students and a teacher and physically wounded twenty-six others.

Columbine High School is located in the southwest suburban area of Denver, Colorado. The building sits where the great plains of the Midwest rise to meet the foothills of the Rocky Mountains. The school opened in 1973; a major renovation that nearly doubled the size of the school was completed in 1995. In 1999, nearly 2,000 students attended Columbine High School. About 158 faculty and staff members were also assigned to the school.

During her junior year of high school, Liz Carlston just wanted to play basketball. She had been a member of

Columbine's varsity team since her freshman year. The morning of April 20, 1999, Liz drove her younger sister Kathy, a freshman, to school. Liz was in her trigonometry class when the shootings began.

Amber Huntington, a shy and timid girl, did her best simply to get through high school unnoticed. During her senior year, Amber worked after school to earn her spending money for a trip to Europe she had planned with her classmates over spring break. Her younger brother, Michael, was a freshman at Columbine. Amber witnessed the massacre in the school library.

Sophomore Michael Johnson was a naturally quiet and reserved teenager who enjoyed hanging out with his friends and fulfilling his church duties. Mike received multiple gunshot wounds; fortunately, none proved fatal.

Mike's mom, Kathy Johnson, worked part time as an accountant. She and her husband, Gary, also had two daughters who were in elementary and middle school in 1999. When the shootings began, she was running errands for her family. Nearly an hour after Kathy returned home, she received a phone call informing her Mike had been shot.

In the pages that follow, these four people each tell the story of their experience with the Columbine shootings, including the tragedy itself and the lingering recovery in their lives.

INTRODUCTION

— Liz —

Hundreds of frightened classmates surrounded me as I sat on a metal picnic table under a concrete pavilion at a park across the street from my high school. I tried to understand the chaos going on all around me. Police cars and officers lined the street to my right. Ambulances and medical personnel rushed across the student parking lot behind the school. Teachers and administrators mingled among the crowd, offering students what comfort they could. Rumors circulated unchecked. But one kept coming back: somebody was shooting students.

I began to look at the school in a new way. The silver metal letters that spelled "Columbine High School" hadn't changed, but now I could barely imagine what lay beyond those familiar tan, cinder-block school walls. Outside the school SWAT teams, dressed in black, held clear plastic shields for protection. Other security officials trained their guns at the school doors and windows. What was happening? Just minutes before, I sat at a desk in my math class. Then the fire alarm rang, and like cattle my schoolmates and I were herded out of the school and across the street. What was I doing here in the middle of a crowd of crying teenagers, surrounded by law officers who seemed to have stepped straight out of an Arnold Schwarzenegger movie?

Those scenes still plague my memory. An unfathomable transformation was taking place; eventually this change would force me to cope with the death and injuries of loved ones, to search spiritually, and probably most importantly, to learn to accept the things I did not cause but could not change. What was taking place around me as I sat on a cold metal picnic table would eventually affect the entire nation and touch the world. Without realizing it at the time, I had crossed over the thin line between innocence and experience. The bizarre tragedy that happens only to other people had happened to me.

1
LIFE BEFORE

— LIZ —

I saw my first Columbine basketball game when I was in the eighth grade. I sat in the crowded gymnasium and watched the team lose. Oddly enough, the experience inspired me, as I realized I could play ball just as well as any of the other girls on that court. I was a competent player, and when I entered the gym in ninth grade for try-outs, I knew I would start on the varsity team. Though that didn't happen, I did start for the junior varsity team and was a reserve player for the varsity team. During my sophomore year, I was named to the varsity team but sat on the bench and watched the team lose game after game. Columbine had had only one winning season in twelve years, and I was watching the losing streak continue.

About a month after my sophomore season ended, the assistant basketball coach, Mr. Sanders, stopped me in the cafeteria with a smile. He told me he had just been named as the new head coach for the next season. I was upset because I thought the program needed an entire overhaul in coaching for the varsity team to be successful. My

Liz Carlston, age 17

attitude began to change, however, as we continued our conversation. As though he sensed my doubts, Mr. Sanders asked about my goals for the next season. I told him I wanted to start varsity and have a winning record. I didn't want to have the reins be so tight on my game time that I couldn't contribute to the team and have fun. With a grin on his face, Mr. Sanders told me he not only thought all those things were possible, but he expected them from me, as a team leader!

That summer, I played on a competitive basketball team and worked even harder at the gym lifting weights. I wanted to become stronger so I could outrebound the competition in the key. When Coach Sanders gave me the chance to play and make major contributions to the team, I planned to be ready.

The 1998–1999 school year began like any other. It was my brother Mike's first year of college and my sister Kathy's first year at high school. And it would be my first year driving to school. I drove Kathy and her friend to school each morning in Mom's white minivan, which we nicknamed "Chester." We had another passenger who always came along for the ride—a yellow stuffed plush doll with a smiling face. We called him "yellow friend," and we kept him safely buckled up in the backseat as though he were a small child along for the ride.

I enjoyed all of my classes. It was a well-known fact at Columbine that Mrs. Theresa Miller, the advanced chemistry teacher, was one of the best teachers. One of Mrs. Miller's class attractions was the tie-dyed shirt each student could make near the end of the school year. Even though I had no chemistry experience, I enrolled in the advanced class.

Mr. Smith was the soccer coach as well as my trigonometry teacher. His class was never dull because you never knew what he would say next. In between working math problems on the board, he would tell us soccer stories or share other random, often funny thoughts.

In world history, Ms. Green gave us maps to plot and showed videos to supplement her class lectures. I had two good friends in history class, Kim and Anne Marie. Sometimes we would entertain each other by making funny faces and then try not to burst out laughing. I had met Anne Marie in a social studies class in seventh grade. We were both in the school band as well—I played the trombone and she played the clarinet—so we hung out sometimes during rehearsals.

That fall, school progressed slowly for me. I was

extremely eager to get started on our basketball season. I was excited about the coaching changes that had been made, and I wanted to show my teammates and the community the brand new Liz Carlston. I felt I had made huge improvements from the year before in my foot speed, outside shot accuracy, and inside post moves. The local newspaper ran a story about what to expect from our team for the upcoming season. In the article, the coach from our archrival, Chatfield, warned her players to keep an eye on Columbine this season because we had made some changes that would surprise a lot of teams. I was happy to read that Coach Sanders told the paper, "The most improved player by far from last year is Liz Carlston." He continued, "She's right at six feet even, and she's put in a lot of time to be better." This was going to be a great season. I knew it! All the frustrations from the previous two years were gone. This time it was just going to be about basketball, victories, and having fun. Coach Sanders decided that since our team of twelve girls had had only one winning season in twelve years, the back of our team's T-shirts should read: "One in a dozen." We were ready to go.

We ended the fall preseason with a record of 3–3, a huge improvement from the year before, when we went 1–5. I remember one home game in particular because I had put off a much-needed haircut, and my bangs were in my eyes. They looked all right when they were curled and styled for school, but after running up and down the court during the game, they straightened out until I resembled an English sheepdog. At one point in the game, I ran down the court on a fast break and a teammate threw me the ball. When I turned around to catch the ball, my bangs flew into my eyes. I completely missed the ball and a chance to score some easy points for the team. Tremendously embarrassed, I ran back down the court to play defense. As I passed our bench, Coach yelled out, "What went wrong?"

"I need a haircut," I yelled back.

A play or two later the other team was shooting a free throw. I was at the half-court line, and Coach Sanders called my name. When I turned I saw him grinning and holding a huge pair of scissors that he opened and closed threateningly. Later that week I went to the salon and got a real haircut.

Games between the Columbine Running Rebels and the Chatfield Charging Chargers were always fun, exciting, and eagerly anticipated by the entire community. Since we had a new coach and a respectable winning record, fans packed the gym to see us play the Chargers in February. The game was close in every quarter; by halftime we were up by two points. Our locker room buzzed with excitement—we could actually win! With less than two minutes remaining in the third quarter, the score was tied. But Chatfield, the defending and favored-to-repeat state champions, stepped up their effort in the fourth quarter and we lost the game. Despite our loss we were thrilled with our performance. We had lost the previous year's game against Chatfield by thirty-three points, but this year we had lost by only nine points.

During practices with Coach Sanders we spent more time on our fundamentals than we had in previous seasons, and players went home tired but happy. Near the end of the season Coach had me practice with the second string team. I was worried that he thought I was not playing well enough, and I asked him what I had done wrong. I promised him I would work harder if only I could play with the first string players again. Coach smiled at me and explained that because I would be his only returning starter for the next season, he wanted to give me the practice and experience of playing with the girls who would be his starting team for the next year.

For the first time in years, the Columbine girls' basketball team actually made it to the second round of the state tournament. We traveled two hours by bus to play against Pueblo South. We were the underdogs, and it would have been a real upset if we had won, but we didn't. They jumped on us early, and we never caught up. I scored only two points in the game, and Coach was disappointed with our loss and our performance. An article ran in the *Rocky Mountain News* the morning after the game. Coach Sanders said our main problem was the other team's tough defense. "My senior [Amber] handled the pressure pretty well, but my junior [me] didn't," he said. I couldn't believe what I read; I was mad that Coach had said what he did. And I was frustrated that in the game the other team defended our post entry pass so well I never got to touch the basketball; I wasn't given the chance to score.

The season was over, but in spite of Coach Sanders' disappointment with our final game, we met our goal of having a winning season. Twelve wins, eight losses—the best in thirteen years. While I was proud of how far I'd come and the improvements the team had made, I knew my senior year would be even better. We were no longer stuck in the mentality of "Why try—we are only going to lose." We had competent players who could handle the ball, and more importantly, we now knew it was possible to win.

After a few weeks off from basketball, it was time to get ready for the summer leagues. On Thursday, April 15, I went to Coach's office in the business wing of the school to talk with him about his newspaper comment about me. Smiling, he greeted me at his door with the news that we would be getting new uniforms for next season. He was excited to show me the catalog and asked for my input. Slightly hesitant to dampen his enthusiasm, I asked Coach Sanders if he was mad at me because of anything I'd done or for any way I'd behaved. He told me he didn't have any problems with me and wanted to know why I asked. I told him how I interpreted the newspaper article. After a few uncomfortable seconds, Coach Sanders told me he didn't mean it the way it was presented in the paper. "I meant it to show your inexperience in big games and be a motivator for you to continue to work hard and improve," he said sincerely.

I felt better after our conversation, and we turned our attention to the upcoming season. We set some goals for the team, and I set goals for myself. Coach reminded me about the team meeting scheduled for the following afternoon. I assured him I would be there. "Good," he said. "You are the senior now, and I want my seniors to be the team leaders." Before I left, Coach told me he had some college recruiting letters floating around in his office. He said he would try to find them for me.

The next day, I was playing basketball at the YMCA when a teammate entered the gym. She asked me why I hadn't attended the meeting. My stomach dropped. I had missed Coach's meeting. I had even promised to attend. I couldn't believe I'd forgotten! I was heartsick.

On Monday, there was a basketball "open gym" scheduled to start at 6:00 P.M.; at open gym we could practice, play, and prepare for the summer leagues. I arrived early because I wanted to smooth things over with Coach. The gym smelled comfortably of polished hardwood, leather basketballs, and mild sweat. Coach Sanders hadn't arrived yet, so I laced up my shoes at the baseline and began to shoot around. Other teammates filtered in and joined me on the court. When the clock approached 6:15 and I still didn't see Coach, I went looking for him.

I found him outside the gym in the hallway. He seemed agitated. I asked if we should start a layup drill. He flashed me an intense look and abruptly replied, "What do you want me to do, Liz?" Jolted by his remark, I turned and went back into the gym. I knew he was mad because I had missed the meeting—the first meeting I'd ever missed in my three years with the program. When Coach finally entered the gym, he sat us all down under the basket.

He started by talking about the meeting. He said he was certain it didn't leave a good impression in the minds of upcoming freshmen when he preached dedication and then they saw how "dedicated" the rest of the team was to not even show up to meetings. The guilt inside of me just kept piling up. I wanted to tell him I didn't intentionally miss the meeting, that I'd simply forgotten, but I doubt he would've listened to excuses; he wanted commitment. He told us if we wanted to remain in his program we weren't allowed to miss meetings or be late for practices, and we must give him a 100 percent commitment. As soon as he said, "No more tardiness," a girl ran in late. He flashed her a sharp look and told us to get up and start scrimmaging. I didn't know what to do. I felt unsettled and scared at the prospect that he might seriously consider cutting me from his program as an example for the other girls. I was angry that I hadn't had a chance to explain myself, and I was annoyed that of all the meetings I could've missed, I'd missed the most important one. Just the week before, Coach entrusted me to be the team leader, and by missing that meeting, I'd let him down.

We scrimmaged against each other for the entire evening. Coach sat on a folding chair at the sideline and watched, analyzing our techniques and tendencies in preparation for the upcoming season. When the time came to leave, I went to the baseline to change my shoes. As I tied my shoes the thought came that I should talk to Coach and straighten things out. Maybe it was my pride or my insecurity, but I didn't even look up to say good-bye. I just walked out the door with the unresolved conflict aching in my heart. I didn't know that would be the last time I would see Coach alive.

— AMBER —

When people ask me, "What did you do in high school?" all I can really say is that I went to school. I wasn't overly involved in activities. The only football game I ever went to was the homecoming game. I liked school and enjoyed my courses and teachers, especially my science classes. I got pretty good grades, although I know I could have gotten higher marks if I had tried a little harder. But I was shy, and I rarely spoke up in class. For me the hardest part of high school was my timidity. It seemed that my

Amber Huntington, age 17

shyness always got in the way of things I wanted to do and how I wanted to be. I didn't feel like I was the person I could imagine myself being—the person I felt I was inside.

Slowly, I started making changes during my senior year. I went out with my friends more on the weekends, I had a part-time job, and I was less afraid of meeting people. I enjoyed spending my senior year with my brother, Michael, who was a freshman. My social successes were due in part to my active religious life. My family was very involved in our church, and I had many friends who were also members. Through the Church, I fulfilled many of my social needs. We had activities every week and dances on the weekends. I was having fun being a social person and started to feel that I could actually handle college. College was going to be an escape for me, a chance to be the person I wanted to be in high school but never was. A lot of growth took place my senior year, and I was looking forward to the future.

I went to England in March of 1999 with my AP English class; I had saved my money for a whole year for the trip. That trip was the highlight of my year; it made it worth it to me to have tagged all those clothes at the dry cleaners after school. After the trip, the school days seemed to pass by more slowly. I was ready to be done.

During the week of April 19, I was looking forward to a party our English class had planned to celebrate Shakespeare's birthday on Friday, April 23. We were each to make a cake and decorate it with our favorite Shakespearean scene; then we would share the cakes with our schoolmates at lunch. If I could just endure my potentially dull week until Friday, all would be well. I woke up Tuesday, April 20, at 6:00 A.M., turned off my alarm, and decided I would rather sleep than go to school that day; after all, nothing important was going on until Friday, and my mom would call me in sick. The truth was that I *was* sick—sick of going to school. I had been going to public school for twelve years, and I felt I deserved a day off. I went back to bed.

I woke up again at 6:50 A.M. with a strong impression that I needed to go to school that day. The impression was so strong I couldn't go back to sleep. The thought that I really needed to talk to my friend Jessica (I called her Jess) kept running through my mind. I didn't know why I needed to talk to her. I just had this unbelievably strong feeling that I had to go to school to speak with her. Fully awake by then, I got dressed and ready in time to make it to my first class.

I had four classes before I could meet Jess in the

library. I was a student assistant librarian during the first lunch period, and I often visited with Jess and her friends before and after my shift. I hoped that by being early I could get a word in with Jess before the librarians assigned me my work. When I walked in, however, I saw I already had a stack of books to shelve, and it was apparent I wouldn't be talking to Jess any time soon. I would just have to catch her after lunch was over. I didn't want the librarians mad at me for talking instead of working.

I picked up my books and began shelving. After fifteen or twenty minutes, I had a strong impression in my mind that I needed to talk to Jess right that very moment. The feeling was so overpowering I couldn't wait. Glancing at the librarians' desk I noticed, odd as it was, that I couldn't see any of them around anywhere. Now was my chance. I motioned to Jess at her table, and she joined me in between the bookshelves. The librarians were gone, so we were free to begin our conversation.

— MIKE —

The night of Monday, April 19, I had planned to stop by the local movie theater and pick up a job application. My best friend worked there and told me he could get me a job there if I wanted one. My dad really wanted me to work there because the managers would be willing to let me have Sunday off. My sixteenth birthday wasn't for another month, so I didn't see the point of applying for the job yet; I decided not to go after all.

Around 6:30 P.M. my cousin called me and invited me over to our Uncle Rob's house to lift weights. I'm naturally skin and bones, but I had been wanting to work out for a

Mike Johnson, age 15

while and so I agreed to go. I hadn't lifted weights much before, so our uncle showed us how and told us we should come over and do different exercises a few times a week. I was excited to work out that night, but for some reason I had a feeling I wouldn't be back. We arranged to go back to Rob's house after school the next day, but the feeling came back even stronger that I wouldn't be back to lift weights. I suspected that my cousin's car would die or something would come up and we wouldn't be able to go.

The next morning, my mom gave me a ride to school and dropped me off in front of the seminary building, which was down the street from Columbine. Mom told me she'd pick me up after school at the same place. Once again, I felt like it wasn't really going to happen. My mom would have car trouble or she'd be late and I'd end up without a ride.

That day a friend told me he knew a secret about the new *Star Wars* movie, which was coming out on my birthday in May. I really wanted to hear the news. I walked with him to his math class on my way to lunch and asked him what he knew. I felt that if he didn't tell me I'd never find out, but he wouldn't say anything.

Every lunch hour that semester I sat on a little grassy hill outside the cafeteria and talked with a few friends. That's where I went after I walked my friend to class. I don't remember if my friends had started eating their lunches yet or not. I don't remember what everybody talked about, either, but I've been told we were talking about religion.

2
APRIL 20, 1999

— KATHY —

Tuesday, April 20, started as normal as every other day. We had to get our kids to school. That year we had three children in three different schools. Gary, my husband, who usually had Tuesdays off, needed to work that day so he dropped our oldest daughter off at Ken Caryl Middle School on his way to work. As I dropped Mike off outside the Columbine seminary building, I don't remember feeling any different or hesitant. He informed me he was going with his cousin at 3:00 P.M. to lift weights at their Uncle Rob's house. I told him I would pick him up after school. I also took our youngest daughter to Leawood Elementary.

I worked for my brother as an accountant. His office was not too far from my home. Tuesdays were usually my day off, but since Gary was working, I figured I would stop by my office and work on a few things. When I arrived around 10:45 A.M., I found my office and work station totally torn apart. My brother thought it would be a good day to move my office around since it was my day off. He

17

Kathy Johnson, Mike's mother

was very surprised I had come to work, but he quickly got my computer hooked up. He then had to leave to work at another location. I was alone, but could not concentrate. I decided to leave about 11:15 A.M.

Both of our daughters had paper routes, so I headed to the strip mall on the corner of Chatfield Avenue and Kepling Street to pick up the papers. I was driving west about two miles south of Columbine High School when I saw a police car pass me on the street. Without warning, I thought, "School." But I had just passed the middle school, and there was nothing going on there. As I crossed the intersection, I could see four police cars far up on the hill, about a mile away; they were close together in a row like a train, racing toward me. My heart started to beat faster. As they passed me, I made a U-turn and headed back toward the middle school. I watched one police car turn north and the other three drive straight ahead. Again I thought, "School," only this time I thought, "Columbine." I wanted to follow the police cars, but they drove so fast they were quickly out of sight. I knew I couldn't catch up with them, so I decided to turn around and pick up the newspapers. I thought again that I should follow the police, but it was too late.

— Liz —

I was tired as I stumbled out of bed on Tuesday morning and decided I would just wear a T-shirt and jeans to school that day. After a bowl of cereal, my sister and I picked up our friend for school. In first-hour English, we had just finished our three-week study of the play *Cyrano de Bergerac.* Our teacher, Mr. Webb, assigned us a detailed project due by the end of the week. We were given class time to work on our projects, and I had the entire thing finished that morning except for an essay describing someone in my life who exhibited the same heroic qualities of honesty, selflessness, and consistency as Cyrano. I couldn't think of anyone to write about.

I liked Mr. Webb because he would let us listen to CDs when we took quizzes and tests in his class. Since we were only working on our projects that morning, he let us listen to whatever music we wanted. The boy who sat in front of me volunteered his Brooks & Dunn CD. While I love country music, the rest of the class could tolerate only one song. I was relieved when English ended because I still hadn't thought of a hero to write about.

After the bell rang, I walked down the science hall to

Mrs. Miller's chemistry class. The school announcements were always broadcast on television during the first five minutes of second hour. The two student broadcasters went through their familiar rundown of upcoming athletic events and school policies. I always looked forward to the quote of the day that followed their remarks. The quotes were not particularly inspiring, but they were something different from the repetitive rambling of the anchors. The quote that day was, "I bet you wish you were not here today." Mrs. Miller made a face and said, "We all do." It felt like the school year would never end.

When I arrived in fifth-hour trigonometry, a substitute teacher told us Mr. Smith was sick and that we would have the class time to complete a homework assignment. I worked on it with the kids around me. The first few problems were pretty easy, but there were two or three problems no one could figure out. We decided we would just ask Mr. Smith about them on Wednesday. I put my calculator, paper, and pencil away in my backpack, which was sitting next to my desk on the carpeted floor. There was a five-foot by three-foot window next to my desk overlooking the park on the east side of the school. I arose from my seat to look out the window. It was a pleasant, sunny day. I decided I would meet Coach in his office after school and talk things out.

The classroom clock read about 11:25 A.M. when the fire alarm sounded. Our teachers typically warned us the day before the fire department would test the alarms. I couldn't recall Mr. Smith alerting us, so the sound of the piercing siren surprised me. I looked around, but my friends were as confused as I was. As I stood up to leave, I glanced out the window. Kids were sprinting across the street and hurdling a fence, running toward the park. The sight of them made me all the more confused. I was one of the last ones to be herded out of the classroom. Down the hall to my left two teachers were shuffling us out and one was crying. Why was she crying? The building's exit was only a few feet from the classroom. Opposite the exit, the main hallway extended to the big staircase that led down to the cafeteria. The library sat to the right of the hall. I wanted to look down the hall toward the stairs and the library, but a teacher behind me instructed us to keep moving. I wonder now, if I had turned my head to look back, would I have been able to see my coach?

I squinted and sneezed in the sunlight when I exited the east side of the school. Walking down the concrete staircase, I looked down Pierce Street where the traffic was backed up as far as I could see. My history teacher, Ms. Green, stood in the middle of the street and directed traffic, allowing us to cross. What was going on? We usually stopped at the bottom of the hill for fire drills, and we never crossed the street.

At a stoplight fifty feet to the north of us, a girl sat on the sidewalk with three adults around her. I saw her leg, bleeding. *She probably tripped,* I thought. *It's not that bad. That's not really blood, but what is it?* We were herded to the large, grassy field of the park. It was there that I first heard the stories from people who had been on the other side of the school. My friend Tyler told me that as he drove back from lunch, he saw a guy with a gun bend over a girl and shoot her in the back. Tyler said it scared him, so he quickly drove to the park.

Kim and Anne Marie, my friends from history, were sitting with twenty other students as they ate lunch on the grass outside the cafeteria when they heard the shots. Anne Marie was shot in the back. Kim tried to drag Anne Marie's injured body away from the gunfire, but she was forced to flee or else she would have been shot too.

Stories circulated throughout the crowd of a fight, of someone trying to blow up the school, of a paintball war, construction, of gunmen in black trench coats killing all the Mormons. I didn't know what to believe. After a few minutes some teachers approached us and told us to move farther back into the park. I sat on a picnic table with a friend who was on the track team with me. We shared what information we knew, and we speculated on what had really happened. We thought maybe there really had been a fire and we wouldn't have school the next day.

By now, hundreds of students had congregated in the park. Suddenly, the crowd ran right toward me. My friend and I ran with them, laughing at the absurdity of the situation. That was the only laughing we did for the rest of the day. When I reached the neighborhood behind the park, I got lost in the crowd. I joined a group of kids who were filing into a nearby house. I sat on the carpeted staircase and watched kids pour through the front doorway and gather in the hallways and living room. A girl came to the door, crying and convulsing, screaming that they had shot her sister and she was dead. Some kids helped her to a couch and gave her a blanket and a glass of water. I learned later who the victims were and was relieved to hear that her sister didn't die. More and more of the kids who crowded into the house were crying and shouting. I had had enough of the madness and tension. I said a prayer asking for comfort and understanding for all who were around me, and then I left the house.

— KATHY —

When I arrived at the newspaper pickup place, the man asked me if I had heard anything about a shooting. He told me a lady who had just left had received a cell-phone call telling her not to go home because she wouldn't be able to get to her house. The neighborhood was blocked off because there had been a shooting somewhere at Columbine. I asked the man if it was at Columbine High School or in the neighborhood, but he didn't know. I was very worried and quickly loaded my papers and left. I didn't know if I should go home or stop by my sister's house. If the shooting was in my neighborhood, I didn't want to be anywhere near the danger. I decided to take my chances, though, and I headed for home.

I sat at the stoplight two miles south of the high school and watched as police cars and motorcycle officers sped through the intersection, one after the other, heading toward Columbine. It was an extremely eerie feeling. I approached the area and saw that my neighborhood was not blocked off. The incident must have happened at the high school. I drove to the seminary building, hoping to find Mike walking home, or at least find out what was going on. I couldn't get down that street; it was blocked. The cul-de-sac closest to the school leading to Clement Park was also blocked with yellow tape, and a crowd of people and cops were there. I asked some boys who were walking down the street if everyone had been let out of school. They were in a daze and told me they thought so but didn't know for sure. Then I saw a group of girls driving away from the school, crying and very upset.

I rushed back home, hoping I would find the door unlocked and Mike watching TV. We live very close to the school. I prayed he would be home, but the door was locked. Mike wasn't home. I immediately turned on the TV. I didn't know what was happening, but I didn't have a good feeling about it. I saw a mom I knew on the television, and she looked very worried even though she didn't have a child at the high school. I felt Mike was in trouble. As far as I knew, he spent his lunchtime in the library doing his homework so he didn't have to do any at home. The reports on TV were saying that some gunmen went into the cafeteria and then up to the library and that people were dead in the library. I kept telling myself it probably wasn't Mike's lunchtime and that he was okay. But I didn't believe it.

I watched for Mike among the injured who were being put into ambulances. I called my friend Heather and asked if her son, a junior, was home with her or if she had heard from him. She said, "No, but I know he's okay." He usually attended seminary at lunchtime unless he decided to eat lunch with the group of guys on the hill and go to seminary seventh hour. But she told me again that she felt he was fine. Then she asked about Mike and I told her that I hadn't heard from him and was extremely worried about him. Heather said, "I'm sure he is just fine," but I said, "No, I don't think so." I wanted her to disagree with me, but she told me to listen to my feelings.

I received a phone call from another friend. She had just talked to her son and learned he was safe in the seminary building. She asked if I had heard from Mike. When I said no, she told me to call her when I heard from him.

I was in constant contact with my mom and my sister Karen during that hour I was waiting. I learned from Karen that Leawood Elementary was the designated meeting spot for parents and Columbine students, so Mom and Dad headed off for Leawood. They didn't get far, though, because the streets around the high school were like a parking lot.

The news reported Life Flight helicopters were trying to land. I could hear the sound of helicopters hovering over my house. For quite some time afterwards, the sound of a helicopter would bring back bad memories. I tried to call my other sister but couldn't reach her. Karen called me back and told me she had learned that parents could also meet their kids at the Columbine Public Library. We debated what to do for a few minutes, and I told Karen to go. She had her cell phone, so if I heard from Mike before she got there, I could call and she would head back to work. I was frustrated because I wanted to be the one to find Mike wherever he was, but I knew I needed to stay home in case he called. I paced the floor. I just wanted to know where he was. About ten minutes later, a little before 1:00 P.M., I did get the phone call, but it wasn't Mike on the other end. It was the chaplain at St. Anthony's Hospital. He told me Mike had arrived at the hospital and that he had multiple gunshot wounds.

— MIKE —

I was sitting on the hill outside the cafeteria when I heard a loud cracking sound to my left. I was a little alarmed, but not too much. I looked toward the sound and saw two men standing about thirty feet away from us, shooting at two kids sitting against the wall. I thought it was some kind of a senior prank and they were just fooling around with paintball guns or something.

Suddenly I felt something very strange and my entire leg went numb. Then I felt warmth wash over me, like someone had poured a pitcher of warm water on my leg. My brain registered that I was in pain, but my adrenaline was high and it wasn't a conventional kind of pain. I looked down and saw that the entire leg of my blue jeans had gone black with blood. The first thing that went through my mind when I saw my leg was, "That was *not* a paintball."

There was a shed at the top of the hill, about a hundred yards from me. I had never took notice of it before, but I had to get away. The bullet had severed my artery, but luckily it hadn't damaged any muscles and hadn't hit the bone, so it was possible for me to run. As I ran up the hill, I felt the same sensation of numbness and warmth I had had in my leg, only this time it was on my face. I heard a kid behind me yelling in a panic that he'd been shot. I realized it might be a good idea for me to do the same. I yelled for help and tried to get somebody's attention. It seemed like an eternity before I got behind the shed. Then I collapsed, completely exhausted.

When I got to the shed, all I could think about was my Aunt Liz. I was four years old when she died in a car accident, leaving five children ranging from four months to six years in age. Our entire family was affected when she was killed. At first I guessed I was thinking about her because it seemed that I was going to die too, and my family would have to survive another tragedy. But then I realized there was more to it than that. It was a miracle that I ran a hundred yards uphill with a severed artery in my leg. It was a miracle I didn't bleed to death within moments of being shot, let alone sometime in the forty-five minutes before I got medical aid. I know someone helped me up that hill. I like to think my aunt was with me, helping me through it.

As I lay behind the shed, I slipped in and out of consciousness. I came close enough to death to feel at least part of what it is like. I sensed a wonderful feeling of comfort. I knew if I died, everything would be okay. I knew it had been the same for my Aunt Liz. I knew she was okay and she was happy. My only reservation about dying was how my family would react. How would life go on for them? I found myself praying, not to live, but that my family would be okay if I died.

The varsity football coach ran behind the shed for his own protection and found me. He got some cops to come help me. While they tried to find a way to get me to the triage center, a couple of students came behind the shed for cover. I remember hearing their voices as they tried to keep me awake, but I don't remember their faces. I found out later one of them was an old friend from sixth grade and the other I knew when we were freshmen together.

Eventually a patrol car came and the police took me to the triage center, which was just a makeshift space in the cul-de-sac at the edge of Clement Park, which is located beyond the athletic fields to the west of the school. I think I was one of the first people to arrive at triage, but I don't remember much there. I remember laying on the ground, looking to my right, and seeing one of the friends I had been sitting with on the grass at lunch. He had also been shot. Someone asked him what his name was, but he couldn't answer them. I told them his name.

I don't know how long I was at the triage center. The next thing I remember was being put on the stretcher and then riding in the ambulance. I've been told that I was awake for most of the trip to the hospital, but I only remember a moment or two.

— KATHY —

I know Mike remembers very little from the time he ran behind the shed to when he arrived at the hospital, but I can testify that something very special happened at the makeshift triage station set up in the cul-de-sac where a member of our church, Linda Madsen, lived. Linda was terminally ill with cancer, and her hospice nurse was at their home when a neighbor came to the door and said someone had been shot. They didn't realize the shooting was from the high school until they went outside and found eight to ten injured students already there and more coming in. Mike was one of those first students at the triage.

Because both Kirt, Linda's husband, and the hospice nurse served as medics in Vietnam, they knew exactly what needed to be done. The nurse asked Kirt to get anything he could to use as compression bandages to stop the bleeding. He returned with towels and anything else he could find from his home. His daughters brought shirts and blankets to help keep the kids warm. They were out there helping before any rescue people arrived. The police arrived first, and then the media, but it took a while before the first ambulance got there. Nearly all the on-lookers just gawked, but Kirt and the nurse gave aid.

Something horrific happened at Columbine High School that day, but I strongly believe the Lord inspired many people to be in the right places at the right time. I believe the Lord placed the hospice nurse at Linda's house, knowing her expertise and skills would be greatly needed. I feel Mike may not have survived if it hadn't been for the hospice nurse.

Both the EMT who attended Mike and the driver of the ambulance were named Chris. They were usually stationed in Golden, but that day they were coming back from Littleton Hospital and were close to the Columbine area when the call came in. They were in the first ambulance to get to the triage center where Mike was. By the time they arrived there were quite a few injured kids, and more people were coming out of their homes with towels and blankets to help. At first Chris was going to take a girl with an injured hand, but then he saw Mike. The hospice nurse had used her stethoscope as a makeshift tourniquet on Mike's leg. As Chris began cutting off Mike's clothing, he realized how badly he was hurt. They tried to get a pulse, but Mike had lost so much blood they couldn't get a pulse anywhere on his body. His face was very pale, but he was awake and could still talk.

The EMT cracked jokes on the way to the hospital to try to keep Mike laughing and conscious. He said Mike was very worried about what Gary and I would think. Chris told him we wouldn't be mad at all and it wasn't his fault. But Mike just kept saying he was really worried. Usually Chris would use three IV bags on the way to the emergency room, but because of an injury in Mike's arm, Chris could insert only one IV.

Mike was on his way to the hospital by noon. He was one of the first students shot, and about forty-five minutes later he was getting the care he needed.

— AMBER —

About five minutes after Jess and I started talking in the library, we heard loud noises coming from outside the building. Most of the students ran to the windows to see what was going on, but we thought it was just construction and continued our chat. Not long after, though, the art teacher, Mrs. Nielson, ran into the library screaming, "Some kids have guns!"

"What? That can't be true!" Jess and I said to each other. We agreed it must be a stupid senior prank. But the look on Mrs. Nielson's face and the tone of her voice as she talked to a 911 operator made my heart start to pound. My mind was in total shock, and I could feel the adrenaline running through my body. I grabbed Jess's arm, thinking we could escape out the back door of the library. All I could think about was getting out of the school. But Mrs. Nielson had received instructions from the operator and screamed at us to get under the tables. She kept screaming until everyone was down. Even though I felt we should flee, we noticed a senior girl motioning frantically for us to join her under a table. Jess and I ran to the table, which was in the middle section of the library but toward the back. We lay under the table, waiting, not knowing what to expect and totally bewildered and anxious. Moments later, we heard the first gunshots from inside the school as the gunmen stormed the halls. I suppose that was when they found Mr. Sanders in the hallway near the library. People started screaming, but we all stayed under the tables. I was having trouble actually believing anything was real until the gunmen entered the library and I heard their voices. Then realization hit and my shock deepened.

As the gunmen entered the library they asked, "Are you guys scared?"

Of course, I said to myself. *What kind of a question is that to ask?* Maybe this wasn't real. Maybe it was just a cruel joke, and they were going to let us go.

I was wrong. It was all too real. They said, "Well, don't be, because you are all going to die anyway."

No! I thought amidst the cries and screams I heard from all sections in the library. *I don't want to die. No!*

I understood clearly how serious their intentions were, although it was still a shock to my brain. *Where are the police?* I thought. It seemed forever since Mrs. Neilson called the 911 operator. *There are usually campus cops around. Why don't they come in and help us? What are we going to do now? This is serious!* I wasn't sure how many students were in the library, but I knew we were trapped. Our attackers, heavily armed, stood between us and both sets of doors. We could neither fight nor flee. We were completely defenseless and at the mercy of two very unstable, inhumane individuals.

There was someone who could help. I was extremely scared and my body trembled with shock, but I knew Heavenly Father could aid me. I held the hands of the other girls under our table and began to pray aloud.

The moment I began my prayer, I felt an instant rush of peace, an emotion of calmness and warmth I never expected to feel in a situation like that. I pleaded with my Heavenly Father. I remember my exact words: "Dear Heavenly Father. We need help. Please help us. I am so scared. I don't want to die. Please help us."

His Holy Spirit told me, "You are not going to die, but you have to endure this. You are not going to die. Just hold on." Although I wished more than anything that I could be instantly transported out of the library, I had faith in my Heavenly Father and I trusted in his promise to me.

From under our little table we heard countless shots ring out. I never realized gunshots were so loud, and I covered my ears. We heard bombs go off and the floor shook beneath us. I remember asking Jessica if those were really bombs and if we might fall through the floor. Everything was total confusion, and the chaotic sounds were intense. The fire alarm punctuated the fanatical ranting of the gunmen and increased the din.

I wondered where the gunmen were because I could see so little from my place on the floor. I barely opened my eyes, afraid of what I might see. I could hear their voices throughout the library, but I wasn't sure what they were doing. The gunshots started to get louder, and I realized they were coming to our section of the library. Then the shots stopped as the gunmen came to our table and set their weapons on top of it.

My heart was pounding. They were right above us. I could see their feet, only inches from my face. Our legs were sticking out from underneath the back of the table because it was impossible to fit all three of us under the table. All the muscles in my body tightened, especially my jaw and my arms.

The whisperings of the Holy Spirit again filled my mind: "Keep your heads down, eyes closed, and be very, very quiet and still." I whispered this to my friends under the table. A lot of other people were crying and screaming, but we were quiet and motionless. The gunmen stayed above us, reloading their weapons and discussing their plans. My heart was pounding so loudly I was sure the gunmen would hear it and try to silence it. My brain was a whirl of confusion. Although I knew I wouldn't die, I was still scared I would be shot, and I tried to prepare myself for what it would feel like and what I should do. I remembered reading an article in a magazine about a girl who got shot in the back while at school. I remembered she said it felt like someone just punched her really hard. I thought maybe that wouldn't be so terrible. I closed my eyes again.

Surely the gunmen could see us! But they seemed not to notice us. It was a miracle. I really believe that Heavenly Father protected us so that the gunmen didn't see us at all.

Then another miracle happened. The gunmen left without finishing their plan to kill all of us. I didn't understand or care why they left or where they went. All I felt was extreme relief and joy as I heard students exclaim they were gone and we could leave.

These were the longest and most terrifying minutes of my life. The room was clouded with smoke and the smell of gunpowder and other bitter chemicals. Finally I stood up and began to run. Unfortunately, I did not check the status of those around me, something I will always regret. I scrambled for the back doors at the far end of the library, following the other students, when I heard the Holy Spirit whisper to me once more, "Run! Keep your head up and don't look down. Just look towards the door and get out." I did keep my head up and never looked down. I am very grateful I followed the Spirit's directions, because I later learned that some of the most horrifying things that happened that day happened in the back section of the library.

— L I Z —

On the street outside the house, I saw three or four kids surrounding one of my parent's friends, Mr. Pollock, who was talking on his cell phone. As I approached, Mr. Pollock handed me his phone and told me to tell his wife I was okay; she would then call my parents and let them know I was okay.

I was confused and not thinking clearly. "Why would she care?" I asked. What was happening? What was going on? Was any of it real? I looked up the street and saw my teammate Cortney get into her car. She was upset and didn't see me. I still wanted to talk to her because I thought she would know what was going on. But before I could talk to her, she slammed the car door and sped away. Who could tell me what had happened? Everyone around me was as confused and disoriented as I was. Alone and unsure where else to go for information, I started the short walk back toward the high school.

Pierce Street was crammed with emergency vehicles. I walked as close as I dared—about a stone's throw away from the front lawn of the school. I watched as law enforcement and other emergency officials pulled a red fire truck up to the front doors of the school. Officers hid behind the truck for protection. I saw two SWAT team members wedge their bodies into the crevices outside the door that leads to my math class. It was a surreal moment. The SWAT team looked as though they were acting in a movie, ready to storm the building and attack the bad guys. I watched as the SWAT team slipped inside the school. I wondered what they would find.

I looked around the lawn to see if I could spot anyone who could answer my questions. I saw Mrs. Samson, the AP English teacher. She had been my older brother Mike's teacher, and I had heard how nice she was to her students. I asked if she knew what was going on, but she just stared at me. I could see that she was as confused as I was. I told her I was worried because I didn't know where my sister Kathy was. Mrs. Samson immediately wrapped her arms around me and said she didn't know where her sister (who was also a teacher at Columbine) was either. Even though we were both hurting and anxious, I felt safe in her arms. Somehow I knew things would work out for both of us.

A few minutes later, the track coach, Mr. Tonelli, approached us. He told us the police wanted all of the students to check in at Leawood Elementary School. I wondered aloud if I should go to the elementary school since I had already left a message for my parents with Mr. Pollock's wife, but Mr. Tonelli insisted I go. As I walked towards the elementary school, I stopped by a parked car on the street with its windows rolled down to listen to the news report on the radio. "There has been a shooting at Columbine High School. We have yet to confirm all of the details, but we have reports that the gunmen are wearing black trench coats. We believe one shooter is . . . " A police officer approached at that moment and told me to go to the elementary school. As I walked to the school I met one of my friends, who told me she couldn't find her sister. Then, as if on cue, her sister ran toward us from a house across the street. I couldn't help but wish it would be that easy for me to find my own sister.

As I turned the corner towards Leawood Elementary, I saw a mass of cameras. Like some kind of celebrity, I had to rush past them into the school. In the main office I saw a girl I knew talking with a reporter. I thought maybe I would be able to learn some information, so I went in the office too. The reporter was from the *Rocky Mountain News* and asked me a few questions. I didn't really have any first-hand information, so I told her some of the rumors I had overheard. I thought maybe I would be quoted in the paper, but as it turned out she didn't include me in any of her stories.

Several parents and students were in the gymnasium. A television sat in a corner next to the stage. I was one of the first students from Columbine to arrive at Leawood and I was anxious to hear more details of what had happened. I flipped through the television channels until I found a live broadcast. Two anchors were listening to a phone call made by a student who was still hiding in the high school. One anchor asked where the student was in the building, but the coanchor quickly told the student not to reveal that information.

Before I could watch any more news, a friend's mom came over and gave me a big hug. She asked if I was all right, and then with tears about to fall she whispered, "Have you seen Carly?" I hadn't, but I knew she had lunch fifth hour, so she had probably been able to get out of the building quickly.

As the gym filled up with parents and students, the mood of the room quickly became chaotic and stressful. I wanted to leave, but I wasn't allowed to go until a parent arrived to sign me out. I had no idea where either my mom or my dad were, when they would arrive, or even if they had received Mrs. Pollock's message. Dad, a systems analyst, worked about eight miles away, and Mom taught English at a middle school about three miles away. I found my friend Gabby and her mom. I was feeling more and more claustrophobic in the gym, and Gabby's mom signed me out so I could leave the building and get some fresh air.

But things outside were just as chaotic as they were inside the gym. I sat on a fence and watched the people around me. I was excited to see the television reporters I had always wanted to meet in person. I thought about going over to meet them, but I knew they would ask me for an interview and I didn't want to talk. I knew I didn't have anything to say. Well-dressed parents used cell phones, calling and searching for their children. On the wall of the elementary school hung sheets of paper listing the names of students who had checked in. I thought my sister Kathy might have checked in, so I joined the mob of people anxiously scouring the lists to find the name of a loved one. Kathy's name wasn't there. Discouraged, I turned away and saw a mother crying. She asked if I had seen her son. I said I hadn't. Almost at that same moment a frantic father pulled me aside and asked if I'd seen his son. "No," I said. Another father asked me if I had seen his daughter. I told him I saw her when we ran into the neighborhood to hide. When I relayed the information, it was as though a great burden had been lifted from him. He smiled and thanked me.

— AMBER —

As soon as I left the school, I saw police officers surrounding the building and a squad car being used as a
blockade. I joined my fellow students, who huddled
behind the police car in front of the athletic fields and
shed. The events in the library were so terrible and
unexpected, I just couldn't process the situation. Kids
everywhere were wounded, but the blood didn't even look
real.

I thought I might have been shot in the arm or somewhere else, since I felt numb all over, but especially in my
arm. I was scared to look. When I finally got the courage
to check my arm and the rest of my body, I was relieved to
find that I hadn't been shot after all. Though I was physically okay, I grieved deeply for those around me lying on
the grass crying. I began to wonder what to do. Other students were helping the wounded, taking off clothes and
using them as temporary bandages. I wanted to help, but I
couldn't get myself to move or think. So I just sat.

Just when I was finally beginning to believe the ordeal
was over, the police yelled at us to lie down on the grass as
close to their car as possible. They thought the gunmen
were on the roof, and the officers drew their weapons. My
heart started pounding again as I lay on the bloodied grass
next to my friends. I prayed that the policemen wouldn't
fire their guns; I didn't think I could bear hearing any
more gunshots. Thankfully, no more shots were fired, and
the men on the roof were gone.

More police cars came across the grass to transport the
wounded students to Clement Park where they could be
treated and taken to hospitals. Since I wasn't wounded, I had
to wait. I understood I should be last, but it was hard to wait

for my turn. I just wanted to go home. I watched the police cars leave with the wounded students packed in together.

As I waited for my turn, a powerful thought entered my mind. My life would never be the same again, and I was scared to go back to my old routine. For a tiny second, I wished I could go back into the library and lie under my table forever. Going back to my old life seemed just as frightening as the whole ordeal I had just undergone. How could I face everyone now, especially my parents and younger siblings? I was breathing, I was grateful to be alive, but I felt my life was over.

It was then that I realized I didn't know where my brother, Michael, was, and for the first time that day, I broke into tears. Like most freshmen, he had lunch in the cafeteria, and I was unsure what had happened in there. The police weren't sure if the danger was past, so they wouldn't let us go back into the school.

Finally, a police car came for the rest of us, and we crowded in. I climbed into the trunk and we drove away. While all I wanted was to get away from the school, I didn't want to leave without my brother. If I could just find him first, then we could go. The police car stopped and we moved into a bigger police truck that was heading to Clement Park. The truck stopped abruptly and we all had to get out. I suppose the police needed the truck more somewhere else. I stayed with two other students: the senior girl who had been under the table with me in the library and another girl who was injured and bleeding heavily from her stomach. We stopped in a field somewhere in the park. The injured girl laid down in the grass, and a fireman ran over to her and did what he could to stop the bleeding. He told us to turn our heads, but I wanted to see. A teacher and a policewoman arrived in a golf cart. The fireman told the teacher he was going to get someone to take the girl to the hospital, and they stayed behind.

The policewoman received instructions from her radio and told us to follow her. The officers weren't sure where the gunmen were, and we had to be careful as we moved through the park; our ordeal was still not over. We ran and hid behind a vehicle in the park. She told us to get behind the tires as she drew her gun. I cried uncontrollably as the reality of the horrible event set in. I wondered if Jess or any of my other friends were injured. I wondered if people had really died back there in the school. I remembered seeing a boy lying on the sidewalk just outside the cafeteria, but I thought he would get up and move. I hoped he did.

The policewoman got another report on her radio that the gunmen might be running through the park, so we hid again. The policewoman told us not to worry, if she saw them, she would shoot them. After learning the report was false, we took off running to the end of the park. The policewoman followed us with her gun still drawn. Maybe now it was over. There were so many police officers and helicopters surrounding the school, maybe someone had finally put an end to it.

A car driven by the school's librarians stopped, and we got in. Since many of the roads were blocked, I couldn't go home yet. We drove over to the house of the girl who had been with me under the table. Her parents were anxiously waiting for her; it made me cry harder just watching them hold each other.

I realized I needed to call home, but I was afraid to.

I'm not sure why. My mom picked up the phone and I said a couple of times, "Is that you?" and "Is Mom there?" She was crying and I didn't recognize her voice at all. Maybe she was afraid to answer the phone, hoping it was her children but fearing it might be a police officer. I asked if she had heard from my brother, Michael. She said she hadn't. I told her I knew he was in the cafeteria during fifth hour, but I hadn't seen him and I didn't know where he was. That was especially hard for me because I am the oldest child. I wanted to protect my younger siblings and be there for them. I told Mom that I didn't want to talk very long because I wanted to go find Michael. I couldn't really understand anything she said during that call. I guess she was just as confused and terrified as I was. Everything was so bewildering. It was like time had slowed down and I was moving in a dream. I knew I was there, but I felt like someone else.

The news was on at my friend's house, and the reporters announced that all the Columbine students were gathering at Leawood Elementary so parents could locate their kids. I told the librarians I needed to find my brother, and they said they would drive me to the elementary school. Many streets were already closed, and we were routed past Columbine again; I had never seen so many police cars, fire trucks, ambulances, and helicopters gathered in one place before. Their presence crushed my lingering hope that this whole thing might not be some major tragedy where people actually died. I recall saying, "As long as nobody dies, I think I will be okay."

— L I Z —

I waited outside the elementary school for an hour before I finally saw my mom. I've never been happier than when I saw her come up the sidewalk. I jogged over to her; she gave me a hug, and asked me what I knew. It wasn't much, and I told her I hadn't heard anything from Kathy yet. She said she hadn't either. We waited outside together for a little while. One of Mom's friends received regular updates on her cell phone from her ex-husband, an off-duty paramedic outside Columbine. By cell phone, he had spoken with their daughter, knew which science room she was in, and wanted to go get her. The mom urged him to let the on-duty officers do their job and for him to stay out of their way.

Whenever a parent or a student screamed or lost control, the cameras would swarm like flies. So many people wore blank looks of disbelief and tears of pain. I felt a worried pain in my heart, so I prayed. I prayed not to be angry with the people who did this. I prayed for comfort and for the safety of those I knew. Not everyone I prayed for came home that day.

Occasionally, a school bus filled with students would pull up to the elementary school. As the busses passed by me, I scanned the faces in the windows. Every time I saw a face I recognized I felt a wave of relief pass over me.

I went back inside the elementary school to get a drink of water, then into the teacher's lounge to watch the news. President Clinton was addressing the nation.

"Ladies and Gentlemen, we all know there has been a terrible shooting at a high school in Littleton, Colorado. I hope the American people will be praying for the students, the parents, and the teachers."

I wanted to hear and see more, but a police officer entered the room and told me to turn off the television. "Why?" I asked. He told me that they didn't want my testimony to be compromised when the cops talked to witnesses. I was shocked when he left. What did he mean *witnesses?* I hadn't seen anything; how could I be a witness?

I went outside to find my mom. She knew Dad was going to the public library to wait for my sister Kathy, but the telephone traffic was jammed and she couldn't get through to him. It was after 3:00 P.M. when Mom called out to me, with a smile on her face, "We've got her!"

Mom and I walked to the car. It was parked nearly a mile away because she couldn't get any closer. The main roads were blocked with emergency vehicles and the side streets were packed with cars, so the trip home was slow. I thought Kathy and Dad would beat us home, but they were still gone when we finally pulled into the driveway.

There were forty-two messages on our answering machine. The little red light blinked frantically. I started to listen to a few messages. One of the first was from my cousin Erin in Salt Lake City. She said, "Hey, Carlstons, what is going on? We saw something about Littleton on the news. Are you guys all right?" Almost all of the messages were from other worried friends and family members. I stopped to wonder how terrible it would have been had everything not been all right. Fortunately, my family didn't have to return any calls with devastating news.

I went into the family room to watch the news. Every channel I watched showed Columbine. It was approaching 4:00 P.M. On the news I saw footage of my classmates running from the school, people screaming, and people crying. I saw myself standing at the elementary school and staring off in disbelief. The next picture showed students running up the school's west staircase with their hands on their heads; I recognized Kathy as one of the taller girls.

While I was watching the news, Kathy and Dad came home. I turned the television off and joined the rest of my family in the living room. Dad had taken Kathy to the local fast food restaurant for a large soda. Kathy was crying and couldn't stop. I joked with her, telling her she had to breathe or else she would keel over. She flashed me a sharp look and kept crying. That scared me because Kathy usually laughs at my jokes, however silly they are. I asked her what happened to her, but she made me go first. I told her I was in my trig class and hadn't seen very much.

It took some coaxing and comforting words before Kathy finally told us what she had seen and experienced. Kathy said she had just sat down with her friends near the center of the cafeteria to eat lunch when Coach Sanders entered the cafeteria from the west side and climbed on a chair. He yelled for the students to be quiet because someone had a gun and that everyone should get down on the floor. Kathy heard a commotion outside and initially thought it was some kind of student prank, but Coach's actions and attitude made her think differently.

Kathy heard a loud pop. Like a ripple, students started frantically to scuttle away from their tables. A second pop rang out. A more intense current of frantic movement ensued. With the third pop, people stood and, like a wave, rushed for the stairs.

When Kathy reached the top of the stairs and entered the long hallway, she had to make a panicked decision. If the gunmen came after them as they ran down the long hallway to the front exits, Kathy, standing well over six feet tall, would be an obvious target. She decided to veer off to the right out of the line of fire and into the science wing hallway.

Kathy's momentum pulled her past one door. She tried the next one. It was locked! Were all the doors locked? Chilled with fear, she hurried to the last door at the end of the hall. When she opened it, she saw the students sitting at their desks. A couple of boys who had been in the cafeteria were telling the others what they had seen and heard. A science teacher came in the room from a side door and told the students to line up against the cupboards and get out of sight from anyone looking through the window in the door. Kathy huddled on the cold floor between her friends Kyle and Betsy.

Moments later, she heard the outside door of the classroom open, and Coach Sanders staggered into the room and collapsed. Pulling himself across the floor with his elbows, he propelled himself behind a table for protection. The door slowly swung shut behind him. For what seemed like an eternity, everyone in the room remained motionless and terrified. The gunmen ran past the classroom over and over again, whooping and shouting and firing shots. The floor shook as explosives detonated.

Kathy sat with her eyes closed, shaking and frightened. Suddenly Mrs. Miller, the chemistry teacher, came in through the unlocked outside door, scaring the students badly with her unexpected appearance.

They heard glass break in the science stockroom next door. Mrs. Miller extinguished a fire that was beginning to spread because of an explosive device one of the gunmen had thrown in there at approximately 11:36 A.M.

When the halls were quiet again, Mr. Friesen went over

to Coach. He saw the blood darkening Coach's blue shirt and asked who knew first aid. My friend, Aaron, and Kevin, who was in Kathy's choir class, volunteered to help Coach. Kathy said almost all the boys pulled off their shirts and gave them to Aaron and Kevin to use as bandages and as bedding to provide warmth for Coach. They applied pressure to Coach's wounds and desperately tried to stop the bleeding. Aaron and Mrs. Miller and other teachers spoke to the paramedics on the phone, receiving instructions and giving specific directions to the science room where Coach lay wounded. The paramedics promised to be there in ten minutes. Time went by. The teachers kept calling. Aaron and Kevin continued to talk with Coach and showed him pictures of his family to keep him awake.

The science room's back wall had a huge window overlooking the parking lot and offering a stunning view of the Rocky Mountains. A helicopter hovered outside the window. A teacher wrote on a small white board, "Help! 1 bleeding to death!" and held it up to the window. The students anxiously waved at the pilot for help, but he just waved back.

As the hours went by, Coach turned a pale blue color. Kathy and the other students were still trapped in the classroom. Not sure what was happening or whether they would live or die, all they could do was wait and pray. Throughout the long hours, the piercing fire alarm continued to echo in their ears. Mrs. Wyatt, another science teacher, offered words of encouragement and held their hands. The students comforted each other. Eventually someone turned on the television where the reports were that twenty-five people had been killed and scores more had been wounded.

Much later, a couple of SWAT team members entered the room from the side door and moved directly to Coach. They ordered the students to line up in single file with their hands on their heads and exit the classroom. After nearly four hours, they were free. Kathy made a point to see if Coach was still breathing when she went past him. He was, but barely. Before they left, she heard him say, "Tell my girls I love them."

The boys wanted to put Coach on a table and carry him out. Aaron said he was not going to leave Coach. The SWAT team man pointed his gun at him and yelled back, "Oh, yes you are!" With laser sights trained on him, Aaron left with the other students as ordered. Coach was alone with the SWAT team men. Aaron later told me how hard it was to wash his hands because all of the water turned red.

Kathy paused in her story and looked at me. She said, "Liz, he's dead."

I snorted back, "He can't be dead; he isn't done yelling at me on the court! Don't worry, they put him in the ambulance and he will be as good as new." I didn't think it was possible that Coach had been taken from us. I wish I could have really believed my own words.

Kathy said that smoke filled the upstairs hallway. Not far from the stairs was a pool of blood. Kathy wondered if it belonged to Coach Sanders. The SWAT team stopped the students on the landing to search them before sending them through the exits. Mrs. Miller wanted to go back upstairs and release other students still trapped in the classrooms but the SWAT team forbade her and ordered her out of the building.

The cafeteria floor was flooded with more than three inches of water from the fire sprinklers. Kathy was hungry and thought about grabbing a bag of chips near the cash registers, but noticed the bags were charred black and blistered as a result of a detonated explosive. Shards of metal and broken glass littered the floor. One of the girls wasn't wearing shoes, so Mrs. Wyatt carried her through the debris.

Outside the west cafeteria door, on the hill to her right, Kathy passed by a lifeless classmate, his face turned up to the sky. Farther up the hill on her left was a friend who lay motionless, still wearing her green backpack. Kathy didn't cry, but had a foreboding sense that terrible changes had been set in motion.

Protected behind the school, she and the other students who had been released from their hiding places in the school were frisked again and then piled into police cars before crossing Clement Park to the public library. Kathy found our dad there and they embraced.

When Kathy finished her story, the tears continued down her cheeks, but at least she had stopped shaking so violently. My family silently sat and stared at the floor, not knowing what to do or say.

— MIKE —

When I got to the hospital, the doctors immediately took me into the operating room. They had to take a vein out of my right leg and graft it into the artery in my left leg. The surgery lasted about seven hours. The next day I had another surgery on my face. The shot I felt in my face actually entered through the back of my neck. It shattered two inches of my jaw and came out above my upper lip. The doctors had to piece my jaw back together and hold it together with metal plates. That surgery lasted about nine and a half hours. I've been told that after this surgery my head was twice the size it usually is and my entire body was swollen. It was only after my surgeries that my extended family was able to see me for the first time.

— KATHY —

I was not shocked at the chaplain's information about Mike's injuries, but I was scared. I must have lost it for a few minutes. The chaplain tried to tell me where the hospital was and how to get there. Nothing registered in my mind. I was shaking and felt absolutely helpless. I knew I needed to write it down or I would be lost and wouldn't get to Mike. "I don't understand what you told me," I said. I wished someone was right there with me and I could have handed them the phone. The chaplain told me to relax and take a deep breath, reassuring me that Mike would be okay. I asked him to just give me the cross streets and I would find the hospital. The chaplain asked if someone would be able to drive me to the hospital or if I needed someone to come and pick me up. He instructed me not to drive myself. I said my sister could be at my house in ten minutes and would drive me to the hospital. The chaplain encouraged me to get there as quickly as possible. I learned later that Mike had told the EMT who was taking care of him on the way to the hospital his name, our names, and our phone number. I believe that is why we received a phone call so quickly.

I called my friend Heather and asked her to call my husband, Gary. I didn't think I could even speak if I had to tell him about Mike; I would have just cried. As we talked, we were interrupted by another phone call. It was Mom and Dad on their way to Leawood Elementary. The roads were totally packed, and they were stuck in traffic. I told my mom Mike had been shot. She was shocked but asked what they could do to help. I wanted them at the hospital, but couldn't see how that would be possible because they had to pick up some of their grandchildren from school.

Karen arrived at my house and offered the use of her cell phone on the way to the hospital. I ended up calling Gary anyway because I realized I had never told Heather which hospital Mike was at. Gary had heard a few minutes before Heather called that there was a shooting at the high school. I was glad I waited to call Gary because I hadn't wanted to alarm him if Mike was okay. Plus, we didn't have a cell phone, and if he had left work to go find Mike, I would not have been able to contact him at all. Gary was extremely calm, but he said everyone at work was hysterical and worried about Mike. I also called my other sister to let her know what had happened to Mike.

Karen and I were driving down the street when we passed Heather, so we went back to meet her at our house. Heather was worried, and since she couldn't get through on the phone she drove over to our house. I decided to call the schools and arrange for Heather to pick up my girls right away. Even though everyone said how difficult it was to get a phone call through to anywhere because of the crisis, I was able to contact the schools before we had even reached the hospital.

When I called Ken Caryl Middle School, they were in lockdown and would not let anyone in or out. I told them my son had been shot and informed them who would be picking up my daughter to bring her to the hospital. I then called Leawood Elementary to arrange for my youngest daughter to be picked up. The office was noisy and chaotic, but I was able to talk to the school nurse, who knew my daughter. My daughter's class had a field trip that morning to the Columbine Public Library and was scheduled to eat lunch in Clement Park before returning to Leawood, but because of the shooting two of the sixth-grade classes were stranded at the library. I finally talked to someone at the library and arranged for my daughter to leave. I am so thankful for all those who helped find our girls and bring them to us.

As we drove through the hospital parking garage, we passed Gary. Karen parked in a no-parking space and we ran into the emergency room where my mom and dad were standing. Having them there was such a comfort. They had been able to get to the emergency room before us because they had been closer to the hospital. Mom had arranged for my niece and nephew to be picked up from school by a close friend.

When we first walked into the hospital, the nurses asked us if we wanted Mike listed under a different name so the media would not bother us. Since we knew the shooting was going to be a big media event, we chose to give Mike an alias. We agreed it would be in our best interest to stay unknown. As a result, we weren't bothered at all by the media. Others who had wounded children had to stay in hotels to avoid the media showing up at their homes and calling at all hours of the night. The hospital was mindful of our feelings and took very good care of us. I am so thankful for the advice and protection they offered us.

The emergency room doctor took us into a separate room. He reported on Mike's injuries and how he was doing. Because his injuries had been so severe, they could not wait for us to get to St. Anthony's before taking Mike into surgery. Mike went to surgery about thirty minutes after he arrived at the hospital.

We were taken up to the Surgical Intensive Care Unit waiting room, where more friends and family joined us. Bishop Mark Severts came to see how everything was going. He told us there were quite a few of our friends' children who were still missing. I could empathize with the anguish those parents were going through. They had no idea if their child was one of the casualties. My heart ached and I hurt for them. The time I had to wait to hear about Mike seemed long, but it didn't compare to the hours of waiting they had endured. At least I knew where my son was and that he was in good hands and being taken care of. I was comforted by those around me. I was told he would be okay, and I exercised the faith within me to know it would be true. Slowly but surely, we received the good news that all of our friends' children were accounted for and home with their families.

Mike was in surgery for his leg for close to seven hours. At first the doctors didn't know if they would be able to save his leg. Later that night, after Mike finally got out of surgery, they let us in to see him briefly before taking him to get X-rays. He was able to open his eyes and see us. I asked him if he wanted a blessing. He barely moved his head, but raised his eyebrows. Gary and my father gave Mike a priesthood blessing. As my mother and I listened, I felt great comfort and knew he would be all right. After the blessing we left him in the doctor's care.

After our family had left the hospital, Gary and I went into Mike's room to be with our son. Sometimes he would get upset at the tubes down his throat and acted like he was going to choke. The nurses would immediately sedate him so he would not pull anything out or injure himself. We stayed with him all night. The nurse brought in two lounge chairs, pillows, and blankets. We tried to sleep, but neither of us was able to because the alarms on the machines kept ringing. It was an extremely hard and long night!

— A M B E R —

The librarians dropped me off outside Leawood Elementary. It was chaotic; there were police detectives, reporters, and counselors along with all the students, parents, and teachers. I saw some of my friends and rushed over to them. We held on to each other as we tried to make sense of the day and share our stories. One friend, Liz Carlston, noticed the blood on my pant cuffs. "Is that yours?" she asked. "No," I responded looking down toward my shoes. We were all asking questions of the people outside the elementary school, trying to learn where our families were and who was okay. Someone said they saw my brother, Michael, run out of the school, safe. Immense relief surged through my body. My brother was okay! My heart broke as I watched other families come to look for their children, only to learn they were in a hospital or still missing. It was too painful to watch, so I went inside the school, where I found more friends. I recall asking, "What are we supposed to do now—just go home?"

By now, more police detectives were interviewing students, trying to find witnesses to the shootings. Since I was a witness, they escorted me to another room. As we walked down the hall, I saw my parents. It was almost like I didn't recognize them. I didn't know what to say or do. I gave them a quick hug and said I had to go with the detectives. They followed and waited for me as I was questioned and wrote down my statement.

It was then time to go home. I didn't want to go, but I didn't know where else to go. My parents walked me out to the car, and I started telling them what happened. They looked at me in disbelief. They saw the blood on my pants. "It's not mine," I said.

We got home around 6:00 P.M. I was tired and hungry since I hadn't eaten anything since breakfast, but I couldn't sleep or eat. I just sat in our family room and watched the news, trying to comprehend what had happened and if it really had happened. The news reports confirmed that some students had died, although they weren't sure about the number, maybe twenty-five, they estimated.

Our phone rang nonstop as friends and relatives called wondering if we were okay. Some people wanted to talk to me, but I didn't know what to say. My brother came home around 8:00 P.M. He had stayed at someone's house across the street from the school until the roads were opened again and the school grounds were cleared. He walked past me, downstairs to his bedroom. I don't remember if we even said anything to each other; we couldn't even look each other in the eye.

— LIZ —

Later that night, Kathy and I watched the news. One of my favorite television reporters was at Clement Park, adjacent to Columbine. As she reported the updates, an explosion suddenly went off in the background. Even that late in the evening, bombs were still going off at the school.

I told Mom I wanted to go visit Coach Sanders in the hospital. Even then, I didn't really believe he would die. She said only his family would be allowed to see him even if we could find him. I insisted she call all the local hospitals and ask about Dave Sanders. As she called, I watched as one of the television camera crews interviewed one of Coach's daughters at Leawood Elementary. She cried and pleaded with the public for any information on William David Sanders. The reporter said he was sure her father was at a nearby hospital and asked the viewers to call in if anyone had any information regarding his whereabouts. Mom turned off the TV when she came back in the family room. She reported no hospital had any patient registered under the name Dave Sanders. She said no one would know anything until the morning anyway.

I learned later that a lot of kids slept with their parents that night. My parents offered, but Kathy wanted me to stay with her. That night I struggled to get to sleep. My mind relived all of the stories I had heard as well as my own experiences from the day. I formulated different scenarios and different actions I could have taken. I remember in one fanciful account I ran down the hallway near the library to where Coach was shot. I knocked one of the gunmen over and grabbed his gun. I shot him in the leg to prevent him from hurting anyone else. Around a corner, his accomplice emerged. I shot him to protect myself and then ran outside to tell the cops it was safe to come in and help Coach Sanders. I replayed the fantasy through my head over and over.

It was 3:12 A.M. when Kathy screamed and sat up in bed because of her own nightmares. I was terrified, and fear chilled through me. She began to cry. I remember holding her until she went to sleep, like I did when we were much younger.

— AMBER —

I absolutely didn't want to sleep alone, but I also didn't want to sleep in my parent's room. I slept with my youngest brother, who was seven. It felt like the stars were falling down from the sky. I didn't know what was real anymore. I felt like my hopes and aspirations were smashed; all my ideas and visions were false. I didn't know what to think of what my world had become. My body and mind were exhausted. I fell asleep instantly, but dreamt about the whole day over again in its entirety, every detail. I woke up and knew it wasn't a dream. This was now my reality. This was my new life, a life in which I couldn't identify with the person from before. Without me even realizing it, an unfamiliar journey had begun.

3
BEGINNING THE RECOVERY

— KATHY —

The following day Mike was scheduled for another surgery for his jaw. Before his surgery, though, Mike's sisters wanted to see him. The girls were shocked when they walked into his room and saw their brother with tubes and machines attached to him, but Mike was really glad to see them. He wanted to hold their hands. When the girls started to cry, Mike did too. He didn't want them to leave. Gary and my father gave Mike another blessing, and then it was time for his next surgery.

When his doctor finished the surgery nine hours later, he showed us the X-ray of Mike's jaw so we could see what he had done. He had attached one long plate and one smaller plate to Mike's lower jaw to help it heal together, and inserted a square plate to help the fracture heal in his upper jaw. The doctor also had to reassemble bone fragments in a two-inch area of Mike's lower jaw. It looked like a jigsaw puzzle. The bullet took out two teeth—a wisdom tooth and a molar. The doctor put arch bars on Mike's teeth so he could wire his mouth shut while it healed.

Thankfully, though, he never had to use those arch bars. Mike's mouth was so stiff he couldn't open it wide enough to get his little finger in. It took many months of physical therapy and hard work before Mike had a reasonable range of motion with his jaw.

We knew Mike was going to be taken off the ventilator on Friday morning, and we hoped he would be awake and alert. I wanted to make sure only Gary and I would be there with him, so on Thursday night I asked my mom to tell our family and friends to hold off coming to the hospital on Friday. We slept that night in an empty room at the hospital.

As soon as we walked into Mike's room at 6:30 A.M., we knew it was going to be a difficult day. We were told he was doing well, and everything was on schedule. We had to leave the room while the doctors removed Mike's tubes and cleaned him up. When we returned, though, Mike was already more alert. The doctors had to remind Mike to breathe because the machine had done that for him for almost three days.

Mike was awake, but he was not happy. He didn't understand what was going on or why he had stuff on his teeth. He didn't remember anything from the past three days. He was very upset. He wanted everything taken off or taken out—now! He tried to do it himself, and when Gary and I tried to stop him, he started to hit our hands away. I called for the nurse. It broke my heart that I couldn't calm him down; I felt so horrible I had to leave the room.

Mike's nurse was able to settle him down. She was a very special nurse. She had worried all night because she knew she was coming to help Mike that day and would be taking care of him. She asked her mother to pray for her all that day so she would be able to handle this difficult situation.

As I cried in the waiting room, I asked myself why I had told my family not to come to the hospital. I had wanted to concentrate on being with Mike and felt it would be a waste of everyone's time to just sit in the waiting room. But now I was alone, crying, tired, and depressed. I felt helpless because I knew that even if I called someone, it would take an hour for them to come. I prayed and asked Heavenly Father to please help me and to comfort me.

I had been sitting in the waiting room for no more than five minutes when Bishop Severts and his friend Brian Thomas (also a bishop) walked in. Bishop Severts sat down next to me and told me he had canceled his lunch plans with Brian because he had felt prompted to be at the hospital. I couldn't speak. Then I saw my friend Heather and two of her children walk in. My prayer had been answered. I told Bishop Severts what was happening and he went right in to talk to Mike, while Heather and Brian Thomas cheered me up.

Heather was the only person I had not called and told not to come that day. She explained that another friend had wanted to come with her, but she felt like she needed to just come herself. If she had taken the time to call and bring our friend, she wouldn't have been there when I needed her. This experience was a strong testimony of how Heavenly Father knows what our needs are before we do. He provided comfort for me through others, who thankfully acted upon their promptings and impressions. Since then, I have tried hard to listen to the Spirit and to act upon the feelings I have.

— MIKE —

The nurses made me drink milk of magnesia, but it upset my stomach instead of helping it. I had arch bars connected to my teeth to help hold my jaw together. They looked like braces, but they were attached at the gum line with hooks that dug into the walls of my mouth. The doctors put wax on the hooks so they wouldn't dig into my gums as much, but they put too much on and I kept swallowing chunks of wax. The wax, on top of my upset stomach, made me gag for a few hours that evening.

That night my entire extended family came to see me. The doctors would only let a few of them come into my room at a time. I remember thinking, "Don't let them in here! I don't want them to have to see me like this!" I thought I looked ten times worse than I felt. I probably did.

I was surprised when I saw how my Uncle Rob reacted. When he first gazed at me, his eyes lit up. He smiled and said, "You look good!" I thought he must be insane to think I actually looked good. What I didn't know was that several of my family members had seen me a few days before, just after my nine-hour surgery, so no one was disturbed by my appearance now. My face had been the size of a basketball then, and I had tubes in my nose, mouth, and stomach. My parents didn't want to take a picture of me when I looked like that because they were afraid it might upset me. I wish they had taken a picture; it would be cool to have it now.

The few memories I have of being in the hospital were definitely affected by the morphine. But in spite of the morphine-induced hallucinations, I do remember different people visiting me. I remember seeing my family, but it felt like a dream. My bishop came to visit me too; he and my dad gave me another blessing. Mike Shanahan, the head coach for the Denver Broncos, even came to visit me.

After the doctors finally took me off the morphine, one of the first people who came to see me was my friend Denny. He was a friend who was with me when the shooting began. He gave me a movie poster, and everybody signed it when they came to visit me. I still have that poster hanging on my bedroom door.

Over the next few days I received visits from more Denver Bronco football players and other people. Terrell Davis came to visit me right after I started to walk again. Walking the three feet from my bed to a wheelchair was exhausting. I could barely keep my head up. When Terrell Davis came in, my dad asked if I knew who he was. I knew his face and under any other circumstances I would easily have been able to say who he was, but I was too tired to remember his name. I think he might have been a little intimidated by me. I must have looked like I was about to pass out. It's probably the only time I'll be able to intimidate a Super Bowl MVP.

The first time I was able to get up and use the bathroom was my first experience at seeing my reflection. I looked in the mirror expecting to see the same face I'd seen for years, but that's not what I saw. The person who looked back at me was a really sickly, little, pale kid with a swollen head and sunken eyes. I wondered if I would ever look like myself again.

— AMBER —

One day after the tragedy my mom was talking to my brother Michael and me. "I dropped you guys off at school that morning," she said. "Why didn't I have a feeling that I should not let you go that day?"

My brother answered simply, "Because, Mom, we were going to be okay."

Then I said, "I wasn't there that day for me. I was there for Jessica." I remembered how strong the promptings were to go to school instead of sleeping in that morning. Those same feelings continued during each of my four class periods leading up to the time in the library. Then only five minutes before the incident began, I felt I had to talk to Jessica immediately. Jessica would have eaten lunch with her friends at their library table had I not motioned for her to come talk to me. Because she was with me when the shooting began, I was able to grab her arm and pull her down with me. As it turned out, three of our friends at the library lunch table were seriously injured, and two girls were killed. It is sad all of them couldn't have been kept from danger.

Sometimes I think of how I didn't want to go to school that day, and how, if I hadn't gone, I would have been spared many difficulties. The main reason I have never been sorry I chose to go to school that day is Jessica. I am very grateful I was able to have the Holy Spirit with me and to receive instructions from that Spirit. It is incredible to play some small part in blessing another person's life.

— LIZ —

The morning after the shootings, my mom drove my sister Kathy and me to our first therapy session with a counseling group set up by The Church of Jesus Christ of Latter-day Saints. We met in the chapel with about thirty other youth. My friend Gabby told me her friend Lauren had died. I told her I thought Coach Sanders was killed too. The counselors spoke to us from the pulpit and directed us to break up into groups of seven or eight people and meet in one of the classrooms. I had already heard my sister's story, so I joined a group of other kids. I wanted to hear where they had been and what they had seen.

In the classroom, our small group sat in a circle. The counselor described the condition of post-traumatic stress disorder (PTSD). He explained it wasn't uncommon for people who have been through a traumatic event to experience nightmares, mood swings, flashbacks, survivor guilt, or hypersensitivity to injustice. He assured us that those feelings were natural symptoms of the trauma, and we were not going crazy in the conventional sense.

It was only in the last few decades that doctors became aware of post-traumatic stress disorder in soldiers who performed their combat duty valiantly, but later were haunted by what they saw and did. The doctors started learning about how trauma can affect a person. Our counselor explained that during stressful, traumatic situations your body goes into shock, parts of your brain shut down for protection, and a chemical imbalance starts to build up in your body. Afterwards, those parts of your brain might start operating on their own, or they might need medication to stimulate them.

Our counselor told us that post-traumatic stress disorder often leads to serious depression, but that one of the best ways to lessen the effects of PTSD is to talk through the experience. He asked us to share how we felt, what we saw, and what happened to us during the shooting. One of the worst things we could do was keep our emotions bottled up inside of us. If we did, the stress and pressure could literally damage our minds and bodies.

The counselor also explained we can cope with trauma by increasing the sense of control in our lives. Something as simple as living in a clean home would allow us to be in control of our surroundings, and we would no longer be a victim of chaos. Many of us were not physically hurt in the attacks, but the counselor said trauma leaves a different kind of wound. While psychological pain does not appear physically, it is still an injury. He said our emotions would travel like a wave. One minute we might be walking on cloud nine and the next minute be mad at the world and the next minute be terribly depressed.

He asked the group who would like to be the first to describe their experience. It was awkward because no one said anything. How could we describe the deaths we saw or the pain we were feeling? Where could we begin? Someone finally broke the ice and shared their story.

My friend Gabby told me later some of the things she was thinking about during this counseling session and the insights she gained from the process. She said:

"I remember the counselor discussed how it all happened for a reason, and things would work out. I wasn't confused about that—I was just mad. I was so unbelievably angry. I couldn't understand how anyone could hurt anyone else like the gunmen did, how anyone could be so consumed in hatred. I was so mad that two people thought they had the right to take someone else's life.

"The counselor asked if anyone in the group was just angry. I shared my feelings with the group and found out others felt the same way. Then one of my classmates said he pitied the two boys. My initial thought was *How could you pity them? They hurt us all!* But as I listened he said he pitied them because if they had only understood God's plan they never could have committed so horrendous a crime. If they knew the judgment and suffering awaiting them, and if they had understood the worth of their own lives, they never would have taken the lives of others.

"In that instant I knew my anger would only hold me back from healing. My anger and fear would consume me until I had nothing left. Even though anger and fear are often natural responses, I knew I would have to overcome them and not give Satan that power over me. In that session I realized that instead of concentrating on my deep grudge, I would have to someday forgive the boys who did this.

"Another counselor told us that even though forgiveness is important, it is also important for us to really understand what it is we are forgiving. He said we are not forgiving the act—we will never view the violence as acceptable—but rather we are trying to forgive those who committed the act. The counselor also gave me hope when he explained that forgiveness doesn't have to be all at once. For something this big it may take us a lifetime to fully reach that level of complete forgiveness. Hearing this helped alleviate my feelings of discouragement. I wasn't ready to forgive, and I'd felt guilty for my feelings. But I soon realized that even though it will take me a very long time to forgive those who hurt me, if I am continually working on it, then Heavenly Father will help me. He understands and wants us to succeed in our trials and to lead us to victory because he loves us so deeply."

The counselors were extremely helpful, but it seemed

the more stories were shared, the worse the details became. There were many terrible things that happened that day, but thankfully, there were also many close calls and miracles. My friend Steven was in the library along with Amber. He hid under a computer desk when the gunmen came in. Whooping and hollering, they laughed about all the fun they were having. Steven said he considered tackling one of the gunmen who came close enough, but didn't because he knew the other gunman would shoot him.

Another girl said that as she began running up the cafeteria stairs, someone told her to go back down and find another exit from the school. She did and that decision probably saved her from witnessing the carnage or losing her own life.

After we made our way around the circle and everyone shared their story, I felt a little relief, but not much. The horror of what other people had had to endure made me sick to my stomach. The counselor told us it was time to break for lunch; we'd have another session in a couple of hours. Like any of us could eat lunch! I could barely stand. I was emotionally exhausted.

I felt a little better after the second session. It was a great relief to share how I felt, and it was as though some pain was taken away from me each time. When we left the classroom a lady handed each of us a comfort quilt. It amused me that high school students soon didn't want to go anywhere without their "blankie"—including me.

When we returned home that afternoon from therapy, we saw several people gathered across the street outside Matt's house. Matt was an athletic, brown-haired sophomore who played football for Columbine. Katy, our next-door neighbor, and my mom crossed the street and heard the news that Matt had not survived the shooting. All I could think about was how, when I was younger, Matt and his little brother would join the rest of the neighborhood kids to play night games like jailbreak and tag with us. And how on the last Fourth of July, my friend David and I went over to Matt's house to shoot off our fireworks. It was hard to accept the idea that Matt hadn't come home from school.

Two days after the shooting I had one of my hardest days. I sat on the couch and watched the news at home. The gunmen were identified as two Columbine seniors, Dylan Klebold and Eric Harris. They killed twelve students and a teacher before killing themselves in the library. Twenty-six other students were injured in the attack. Coach Sanders died in the arms of a SWAT team member in the science classroom. I was impressed that he was able to hold on to life until all of the students had left the classroom.

The two gunmen had set up a propane tank bomb in the cafeteria only ten feet from where my sister Kathy sat for lunch that day. After the cafeteria had been evacuated, the gunmen took potshots at the propane tank with their rifles. Their original plan was to detonate the bomb during the busiest lunch hour, killing more than five hundred people, and then pick off the survivors with their guns. Why didn't those propane bombs go off as planned? I believe angels were there that day; I believe it was divine intervention.

Some news reports said the gunmen's actions originated because they were picked on and ostracized. I didn't know either boy personally, though Dylan had a PE class the same hour I did, but I feel that they lost sight of reason and reality, harbored hurt feelings, and chose to surround themselves with malicious influences. I pity them both because the foundation of evil on which they based their actions crumbled, leaving them with nothing. From their actions, I learned it is far better to suffer than to cause the suffering.

That Thursday, the news broadcast the names of the thirteen people who had died and those who had been injured. I already knew Coach and the boy across the street, Matt, had been killed. I learned that my friend from history, Anne Marie, was in critical condition with gunshot wounds to her back. Her injuries paralyzed her from the waist down. I was too scared to visit any of my friends who were in the hospital. I didn't know what to say, and I was unsure of what I could have offered beyond a smile or kind word. Looking back now, I understand that that may have been all that they needed.

When the names of the victims were released, I cried. Earlier that month, I had said a short good-bye to my brother as he left for his mission to the Czech Republic. I cried then because I knew he would be gone for two years and he would miss my senior year of basketball, my graduation, and my first year of college. I was crying now because I had to say a long good-bye to Coach. He was not going to be at any more practices or games; he was gone.

My heart ached. I didn't know if I was really sad or if I was just crying because it seemed to be expected of me. I felt overwhelmed with guilt. Why was I allowed to live while so many others were killed or injured? Why didn't I do more to help than what I had done? I couldn't feel anything. I was numb. I didn't feel comfort anywhere; I didn't feel safe anywhere. And eventually I just felt nothing at all.

Coach's name and photograph flashed across the airwaves, and I stared at his face as though he could see me. I tried to decide if he was still mad at me for missing the basketball meeting. I didn't know what else to do, so I prayed. I asked if I could feel at peace and if I could have the strength to continue on and not give up. I prayed for Coach's family and for all the other families who had lost someone. I know the Lord heard my prayer.

All of a sudden I felt an urge to let Mrs. Sanders know how much her husband meant to me. I pulled out a card and a pen and wrote down one of my memories of Coach. I wrote about a bus ride home from a road game. A teammate and I had our headphones on and we broke out in singing an off-pitch version of Faith Hill's song "This Kiss." We got mean looks and rude comments from other teammates who wanted us to keep quiet. But Coach just bit his tongue and later made some funny one-liner comment about how we were turning into basketball-playing divas. I mailed the letter to Mrs. Sanders.

An informal gathering at a local church's auditorium was held Thursday evening for all the students. I went with my mom; Kathy didn't feel like going. It was good to see so many of my classmates again. Our principal, Frank DeAngelis, looked haggard. An area administrator stood up and gave us some general information about what was going on and what would happen to us. She said we would finish the school year at Chatfield. I was stunned to hear that not only were we expected to finish the school year, but that we would be attending our rival school!

The administrator told us that we would not be able to

attend school at Columbine until the next school year began in August. She concluded by saying, "All of our hearts are aching because of the tragedies that occurred on Tuesday at *Chatfield High School.*" The crowd was silent. Then people started to boo. It was a horrible mistake to make in front of a crowd of traumatized Columbine students who still had their school pride. It was worse than a slap in the face. She quickly finished what she had to say and hurried to her seat.

Principal DeAngelis stood up and the place erupted with cheers. It didn't matter what he said. Just having him there encouraged us to be strong. Some girls in the balcony began to chant "We are . . . ," and the rest of the crowd finished by yelling "Columbine!" Back and forth we chanted: "We are . . . Columbine!" Our hearts were breaking, but our spirits were strong. I started to cry, and I couldn't stop. Tears still fell uncontrollably as I left the meeting with my mom.

It was nearly a week and a half after the shootings before I was allowed to pick up my car from the school's parking lot. Purses and other valuables belonging to teachers and students were still locked up in the school. That day, my mom and dad dropped me off at the seminary building about a block away from the student parking lot. It had snowed the day before, so the sidewalks and streets were slick with ice. As I walked up the hill, I looked at the school with fear and apprehension.

I was nervous approaching my faithful minivan "Chester" because I knew the gunmen had also placed bombs in their cars. Even though the police had searched our cars, I was afraid they might have missed a bomb hidden in the yellow doll I kept in the backseat. When I opened the sliding door, I very cautiously pulled my yellow friend from his seat belt. Terrified, I opened his back and was relieved to find only batteries. I chided myself for being so naïve and jumpy. While I scraped the ice off the frozen windows, a police officer watched me from her patrol car. She was probably suspicious as she watched me dig around in a yellow stuffed doll's body.

I turned Chester's ignition and rounded the corner to the student's back door entrance. I wondered what lay behind those cold doors. The police hadn't allowed the school to be cleaned because it was still a crime scene. Our backpacks were locked up inside as evidence. Although I had been there, I desperately tried to comprehend fully what took place behind those icy doors. I could understand why some of the kids said they never wanted to go inside Columbine again and that the school should be torn down. It was a haunted place now.

The time came for the funerals. I made up my mind that I would attend only two: my neighbor Matt's and Coach Sanders's. Even though I knew some of the other kids who were killed, it was too much of an emotional roller coaster to endure all the sorrow and pain as family and friends reminisced about the life lost and what might have been. On Tuesday, April 27, my family went to Coach's funeral. It hurt too much to think about where I was going and who I would see lying there in the casket, so I went with a blank mind, void of thought or emotion. I knew if I started to think about him, I would break down and cry. Coach Sanders's funeral was held in a church building filled to capacity by the 2,500 people who came. The basketball team sat together, and the Sanders family sat in the front with friends and faculty from Columbine.

It hurt to be there. Coach's casket held true to the Columbine colors of navy blue and silver. I cried through most of the service. People who knew him best were asked to get up and share their favorite memories, something for the Sanders family to remember. The experience left me sad and depressed because it felt like everyone was saying good-bye forever. I've always believed there is a life after death and we will see our loved ones again. How could it be otherwise? Why would God allow us the joy and pleasure of loving our friends and family only to take them away from us forever? The world makes death seem like a permanent separation, but I know God loves us too much to let death be the end.

When the last prayer was given, we were invited to walk past Coach's open coffin to say our final good-byes. When my turn came, I saw he was wearing his orange basketball tie. It was his good-luck tie, and he always wore it to our home games because he said it helped us play better. Coach looked different. It wasn't just the makeup on his face. He seemed smaller.

I left my basketball letter—a little pin that went on my letterman jacket—with Coach and walked away. I felt I was leaving my passion for basketball behind too. I did play the next season, but my focus had changed. Basketball suddenly became a trivial recreation in the grand scheme of life. I felt I needed to place my efforts elsewhere. My senior year I played without the same passion and dedication for the game as I did when Coach Sanders was alive. I didn't play the game for fun; I played it for Coach's memory and to finish four years with the program. Even though I enjoyed some real success, it was my toughest season.

My math teacher, Mr. Smith, stood a distance away

from the casket and watched me walk away from Coach. He saw the pain in my face and cried himself. His look seemed to say, "This is not fair. Why should anyone have to go through this?" I've often wondered the same thing.

My dad told me a story to help me deal with the loss. He reminded me of the days when people crossed the ocean on large steam-powered ships. When the ship left the harbor, people would line the docks and shed tears as the ship grew smaller on the horizon. But at the receiving harbor, the people would line up and cheer as the ship grew larger on the horizon and eventually arrived at the dock. Dad said that is like what happened to Coach. We all cried tears of sorrow as he was taken from us, but I am sure the hosts of heaven gave shouts of joy when greeting him as he walked through the veil of this life into their view.

A few days after the funeral I felt another urging to visit Mrs. Sanders. I had little idea what to say to her, but I knew she would probably want to hear from some of her husband's players. Before April was over I gave her a call and arranged for a visit. I only knew her by face, so I was absolutely terrified about what to expect. Her feelings were very fragile, and I only wanted to offer her the support and knowledge that she was not alone and to share my condolences and memories. I called Cortney, a friend and teammate, to go with me because I knew she felt the same way as I did about Coach.

Mrs. Sanders was very gracious and friendly as she welcomed us into her home. We shared stories about Coach and cried with each other. I asked her what she thought about all of the media attention. She told us her privacy was constantly being violated. A news truck would spend evenings parked in front of her house with cameras pointed at her windows. More than once, a reporter and photographer were caught climbing over her backyard fence. In the grocery store a lady who recognized her approached and asked her to autograph a magazine story about her late husband.

I continued to visit Mrs. Sanders with different teammates about once every two weeks. One night I called her for permission to go over and visit. As the phone rang, I stood in the living room. The room grew cold as the sun set behind the mountains, leaving the room fairly dark. When Mrs. Sanders answered the phone she was crying. I asked what was the matter. She told me she was just missing Dave. After a few seconds of silence I said, "I don't know what to say." She tearfully responded, "I wouldn't know what to say to me, either." I ended up telling her I was praying for her and to just keep going. When I hung up the phone I went to find my mom. I cried into her shoulder.

Why was I so powerless and useless to help someone who felt so much pain? Why was I hurting so much? Would life ever be normal again? I didn't know the answers to any of my questions. The only things I could do were to pray for her and to talk with her. Psalm 147:3, 5 came to my mind: "He healeth the broken in heart, and bindeth up their wounds. . . . Great is our Lord, and of great power: his understanding is infinite." I put my faith in God that all would be well. I felt assured all things happened for a reason and he knew how I felt and how Mrs. Sanders felt. I experienced his comfort and calming hand when I sought it.

I met with Mrs. Sanders only a few additional times in

the months that followed. It is strange to realize that while I went to her to offer her comfort, she probably helped me more than I helped her. I don't know how much consolation I was able to offer Mrs. Sanders, but by allowing me into her home, she made me feel as though I helped relieve some of her pain. She helped me forget myself and my own pain as I tried to comfort her. I was able to leap beyond my own solitude and sulking and show her Coach Sanders had made a difference and had left a positive impact on my life.

On May 3, just two weeks after the shooting, we began school at Chatfield. Class was held from 1:00 P.M. to 5:00 P.M. Since the Chatfield students attended class in the morning, they were gone by the time we arrived. The first day of school, I parked Chester in the student lot and saw the hoards of media people crowded on the opposite side of the street. For security reasons we were required to wear school ID cards around our necks. Parent volunteers greeted us at the doors before school started each day to check our ID cards.

We entered the school and were welcomed by a hallway decked out with posters from all over the country offering words of support. The posters were also strategically placed to hide Chatfield's glass-paneled library windows. The trauma of a library was still very much alive in all of us. We met in the gym for an assembly where guidelines were provided about how classes would be conducted, what was expected of us, and where support services would be located. Classes the first day back were somber and depressing. It was good to see friends again; yet sad because we knew some of our classmates were missing and things were different. We all had lost a piece of our innocence and found ourselves in a new dimension of life.

Following the assembly I went to my trigonometry class. Mr. Smith told us about his experience on the day of the shootings. He was home sick with his young daughter. As he flipped through television channels, he caught sight of a special report. He was shocked to learn about the shootings. He admitted it was a good thing he hadn't been at the school because he probably would have rushed in and done something stupid to stop the killers. After Mr. Smith finished speaking, he asked us to write a letter to the parents of a classmate who lost his or her life. He told us even if we didn't know the other student very well, any memory we had of them would be of value for the grieving parents. I wrote to the parents of Kelly Fleming. I wrote how I saw her at lunch a few times and shared my memory of her shy smile.

I was most eager to move onto Mrs. Miller's class, my chemistry teacher who worked to save Coach's life. Like all of the teachers, she told us her story during class. After class I asked her what she knew of Coach Sanders's last few hours. I wanted to know if Coach could have been saved, if there really was no way to have prevented his death. She told me medical personnel informed her that the type of wounds Coach had suffered needed to be treated within the first ten minutes. I asked her why the EMTs had not arrived to help him sooner. She said while they were trapped in the classroom, she or other teachers were on the phone nonstop with the emergency dispatcher, who repeatedly said someone was on the way. Coach didn't die alone. With tears about to fall I asked, "Couldn't someone have held his hand?" Mrs. Miller told me there wasn't time; they fought for every second to keep him conscious, alert, and alive. Mrs. Miller answered all of my questions with patience despite the obvious pain she must have felt.

One day while I sat in class at Chatfield, I began to stew over all the circumstances that had gone wrong in my life. I relived all of the injustices I'd experienced. I'd never been a bad kid. I did what I was supposed to do. I got good grades, worked hard, stayed away from alcohol and other damaging substances and situations. I didn't deserve what happened to me. But after digging myself a deep pit of pity, I was even more miserable. I tried to understand why these bad things happened, but instead of focusing on finding guidance and answers from God, I kept dwelling on all the times my life didn't go the way I wanted it to. I learned that it's easy to find something wrong with the world, to be angry and unteachable. It's easy to be focused only on one side of the spectrum and overlook the good still left.

It was only when I started to look at the other end of the spectrum and to count my blessings that my anger began to ease away. Though I'd heard it a hundred times, I began to understand how bad things can happen to good people. I realized that great people are those who endure their challenges without complaint or self-pity. They instead rise to the challenges and face them as best they know how, though uncertain of the consequences or results.

Following the shootings there was a tremendous outpouring of goodwill from the nation in the form of prayers, banners, cards, and flowers. Though I recognized and appreciated the support, the distance of many of the writers and the impersonal nature of their letters made these offerings feel remote and insufficient to heal my heart. Instead, I tried to identify other blessings the Lord had given me, and I realized my most unique gift was right before my eyes. I had my family. Though we have our problems and are far from perfect, we love each other and are there for one another. As my family and friends shared stories of overcoming adversity in their lives, they were able to act as guides to lead me away from the anger, guilt, and doubt I was still experiencing.

My Aunt Karen called my sister Kathy and me from Wyoming nearly every night for weeks. Her supportive calls were a constant motivation for us to move forward. Aunt Karen played the role of a sounding board and encouraged us to talk about whatever crossed our minds. She just listened as we rambled through our thoughts, trying to process what happened to us. She didn't have to call us every night, but she did; and since she did, we knew we were loved and that things would eventually be okay.

We all have blessings. There is always something somewhere to smile about. With all the blessings the Lord has given me, I know he loves me. His love showed me I could fully trust him. As I inventoried all the gifts my Heavenly Father had given me, I was humbled at the abundance. I needed to do something good with the blessings he had bestowed upon me. I needed to start by overcoming my depression, by accepting my reality and not allowing it to consume me. I knew it would take time, but I was determined to make it happen.

With all the heroic acts performed by the ordinary people in my life that spring, the selection of a hero for my English essay should have been easy. Teachers, students, emergency personnel, parents, and other people all around me exhibited those characteristics that define a hero. Mrs. Miller did the best she could to save Coach's life. Mrs. Samson calmed a frightened student in the park with a hug. Emergency workers treated injured students immediately after the shootings began. Kim tried to save Anne Marie by moving her away from the gunfire. Without giving second thought to their own safety, these heroes sacrificed part of themselves without the promise of glory, money, or accolades. They did what they did because it was the right thing to do. They were the right people in the right place at the right time. Many more students would have been hurt had Coach not been where he was, when he was. Coach Sanders left this world saving people he didn't even know. The good choices he made prior to April 20 put him in a position to save many people. We, too, are empowered with the ability to make our own decisions, and hopefully we will choose to strengthen the world by adding light and goodness to it. The people that we are and the simple things we do all have impact and purpose.

4
LEARNING HOW TO HEAL

— KATHY —

As the days passed, we saw great improvement in Mike. We knew there would still be many challenges and hurdles to overcome, but we were encouraged every day that Mike felt better and showed signs of improvement. I feel his positive attitude and desire to get better had a huge impact on his recovery. So, too, did the many prayers that were said on Mike's behalf that day and in the months following.

Mike and I have discussed many times how blessed he was to be spared the emotional traumas others had. He was one of the first to be shot outside and so was not trapped within the school walls. He didn't have to hear the alarms ring for hours. He didn't have to experience the horror so many others did, or see someone shot to death right next to him, or have to plead for his life. He didn't have to wait for hours wondering if he would ever be rescued. He didn't have to listen to gunfire or bombs exploding and wondering if the shooters would find him. He didn't have to watch a teacher suffer and bleed to death. He was physically injured, but he was so blessed with the doctors who took care of him.

Months later, as I watched the taped events of that day unfold again, I cried every time I watched parents meet up with their children. I was sad I could not find my son safe and physically unharmed the way they did. But then I am overwhelmed with gratitude because I still have him here to talk to and be with. Mike is a survivor. His mission upon this earth is not complete. As I think about the events of that day and how it changed our family's lives forever, I hope we have learned from our trials how to help those people who cross our paths in some way and how to be more tolerant of one another. We are all different, and we need to be more accepting of our differences.

I pray each day to a loving Heavenly Father, who knows what I need and who has helped me make it through many challenges in my life. I have learned and grown greatly in the years after Columbine and know I could not have made it through without the knowledge of the gospel of Jesus Christ. I am so thankful for his atoning sacrifice, for the Holy Ghost, and for my family and friends. I have been blessed by all three throughout the trials in my life and continue to pray for strength to endure to the end.

— MIKE —

I was released from the hospital after eight days. My family threw me a welcome home party and ordered pizza. I was upset I couldn't eat it. I was on a strict milk shake-consistency diet for the first few months (every kid's dream for the first week, every kid's nightmare after that).

I was supposed to use crutches to help me walk, but

Mike Johnson, age 19

they were so cumbersome that after a day I went to a cane. About four days after using my cane, I decided I'd rather limp around on my own. Six weeks later I finished physical therapy on my leg and could walk and run normally again.

I had physical therapy for my mouth as well, and that process was a little more exhaustive. The muscles in my mouth had tightened up until I could open my mouth only about ten millimeters—not even wide enough for a peanut M&M. During those sessions my therapist would basically force my mouth open. It was painful, and I had to do it for five months.

I feel blessed because my emotional health was actually very sound. I only had one minor post-traumatic episode. I went to my cousin's baptism about two and a half weeks after the shooting. Town houses were being built behind our church building, and someone was using a nail gun. I knew it wasn't a real gun—it didn't even sound like a real gun—but it was similar enough to trigger my instincts to get away as quickly as possible. I knew I wasn't in any real danger, so I forced myself to remain calm and enter the building. As everybody else went to the font area, I went to the Primary room instead and cried. My mom found me and helped me calm down in time for the baptism.

As I look back now at being shot, I realize something about life. The most difficult aspect of remaining happy during hardships is having an eternal perspective—remembering there is something beyond the veil, something more than this moment of our existence. We have faith God is there, and when we feel his love from time to time, we can experience a solid confirmation that what we've been taught is right. But when those moments leave and we are left with only our memories of them, we sometimes forget that deep sense of conviction.

A lack of eternal perspective can lead us to mourn death or resent hardships to the point of self-pity and depression. If we remember our faith and the love God has for us, we can be assured our deceased loved ones really are waiting for us on the other side of the veil. But there is more to maintaining an eternal perspective than realizing our deceased loved ones are in a better place. When Joseph Smith was in Liberty Jail, he asked God the same exact question we often ask him about our distress. The Prophet's cry is in Doctrine and Covenants 121:1–6.

> O God, where art thou? And where is the pavilion that covereth thy hiding place?
> How long shall thy hand be stayed, and thine eye, yea thy pure eye, behold from the eternal heavens

the wrongs of thy people and of thy servants, and thine ear be penetrated with their cries?

Yea, O Lord, how long shall they suffer these wrongs and unlawful oppressions, before thine heart shall be softened toward them, and thy bowels be moved with compassion toward them?

O Lord God Almighty, maker of heaven, earth, and seas, and of all things that in them are, and who controllest and subjectest the devil, and the dark and benighted dominion of Sheol—stretch forth thy hand; let thine eye pierce; let thy pavilion be taken up; let thy hiding place no longer be covered; let thine ear be inclined; let thine heart be softened, and thy bowels moved with compassion toward us.

Let thine anger be kindled against our enemies; and, in the fury of thine heart, with thy sword avenge us of our wrongs.

Remember thy suffering saints, O our God; and thy servants will rejoice in thy name forever.

Joseph was asking God why he wouldn't help him in his moment of despair. Joseph and others had been unjustly imprisoned in Liberty Jail throughout the winter. They suffered a great deal of physical pain and didn't have much hope of being released. Our ordeals are different, but our cries for help are similar to Joseph's. God's answer to the Prophet in Doctrine and Covenants 121:7–9 is both helpful and comforting.

My son, peace be unto thy soul; thine adversity and thine afflictions shall be but a small moment;

And then, if thou endure it well, God shall exalt thee on high; thou shalt triumph over all thy foes.

Thy friends do stand by thee, and they shall hail thee again with warm hearts and friendly hands.

When we are dealing with trials, it's easy to feel like our adversity will last forever, but when we have an eternal perspective, we realize our problems last "but a small moment." If we remember this truth and bear our trials well, we can be with our loved ones again. If we forget and begin to dwell on our losses, we will become depressed and possibly lose our faith in God. Because of my experience on the hill near Columbine, I know death is not the end. Most people have faith there is life after death, but I have come to *know* life is eternal. I know there is a God. I know he loves us and wants us to be happy.

I know I have been blessed with a washed memory. I remember being so frustrated when I got home from the hospital because literally every memory I had of the two months before the shooting was totally mixed up. Not one memory had a time stamp on it. I remembered things that had happened—I just couldn't remember *when* they happened. Yet I think the fact that I remember so little about the shooting itself and about the days surrounding it helped me overcome the emotional hurdles of the trauma.

I know keeping an eternal perspective has helped me survive. It is a wonderfully comforting thought that no matter what we go through in this life, God is on our side. He wants us to come back to him more than anything, and if we endure to the end, remembering the love he has for us, we will be happy for eternity.

I know God blesses our lives. We are given trials in order to grow. The specific trial given to me was difficult to endure, and no one who was involved in any way with my trial has been the same since. That is the nature of trials. They change us and mold us into who we are. Whether that change is good or bad is up to us.

I saw many people who were not able to forgive and who were harboring feelings of hatred toward others and themselves, instead of focusing their energy on forgiveness and healing. As a result, they became bitter, lonely, and depressed. They were unable to overcome their trials.

I saw others who tried to take advantage of their own misfortune and the charity of others in an attempt to gain money and material possessions. They became so involved in getting what they wanted that they forgot to be mindful of what they needed. They didn't focus enough on their own healing and ended up miserable as well.

On the other hand, I saw people grow from the experience. I witnessed people unite to help each other survive a difficult time. I personally feel like my trial turned into a blessing. I'm not saying I'm glad it happened—the crimes that were committed against us could never be justified—but I know the bad things that happened to me were outweighed by the growth I experienced as a result. I'm thankful for the personal and spiritual strength I developed as a result of this tragedy.

I'm so thankful for a Heavenly Father who loves me. I'm thankful for the restored gospel and the wonderful influence it is in my life. I know that Christ lives. I know that he died for us and was resurrected. He suffered so much more than any of us can even possibly imagine so that we may live with God forever. I love him with all my heart and intend to serve him for the rest of my life.

I'm thankful for my trials. I know that if we turn to God in everything we do, we will be happy. I hope that by sharing my experience, I am able to testify that it is our faith in God that will help us in our times of trial. As long as we put our faith in God, he will never let us down.

Liz Carlston, age 21

— L I Z —

On May 20, 1999, high school students from Columbine, Chatfield, and Dakota Ridge were invited to Dakota Ridge High School to meet the president of the United States. My sister Kathy stayed home because, as she put it, she didn't want to be a part of a photo opportunity for President Clinton. I didn't care if it was a photo op or not. This was the *president.* We were released from school early so we could attend.

When we walked around Dakota Ridge to the designated doors, we saw Secret Service agents waiting in front of metal detectors. For security reasons, we weren't allowed to bring anything inside with us, not even a pen. I was disappointed because I had wanted to get the president's autograph. A wooden podium with the familiar presidential eagle insignia stood on a temporary stage at the front of the gym. I found a seat in the bleachers with some friends. The air was filled with excitement and anticipation of seeing the president.

To pass the time while we waited, we entertained ourselves with cheers and chants more commonly found at a basketball or football game. Colorado's governor, Bill Owens, sat in the bleachers with the student body and even joined in with our calls. After thirty minutes, the president, Mrs. Clinton, and our principal came on stage. When Principal DeAngelis stood to introduce the president, he was met with roaring applause and shouts of praise. Before President Clinton spoke, the president said, "Do that cheer for me one more time." He then addressed the students.

"When America looks at Jefferson County," he said, "many of us see a community not very different from our own. We know if this can happen here, it can happen anywhere. And we see with admiration the fundamentally strong values and character of the people here, from the students to the school officials, to the community leaders, to the parents. . . .

"We know somehow that what happened to you has pierced the soul of America. And it gives you a chance to be heard in a way no one else can be heard—by the president and by ordinary people in every community in this country. You can help us to build a better future for all our children, a future where hatred and distrust no longer distort the mind or harden the heart. A future where what we have in common is far more important than what divides us. . . .

"A future where society guards our children better against violent influences and weapons that can break the dam of decency and humanity in the most vulnerable of children. . . .

"The older you get, the more you'll know that a great deal of life is the struggle against every person's own smallness and fear and anger—and a continuing effort not to blame other people for our own shortcomings or our fears."

President Clinton reminded us that just that morning there had been another school shooting in Atlanta, Georgia. My heart dropped, and I saw despair on many of my classmate's faces. Hadn't anyone learned anything? Couldn't people see how much pain and anguish there is when a school is attacked? Shooting someone doesn't solve any problems. President Clinton continued, "Thankfully, the injuries to the students don't seem to be life-threatening."

He concluded his speech with a story about Nelson Mandela. Mandela served a prison sentence lasting more than twenty-seven years, laboriously breaking rocks every day. He was separated from his wife and children and was physically and emotionally abused. President Clinton said that he had asked Nelson Mandela, "How did you let go of your hatred?" In response Mandela said, "One day I was breaking rocks, and I realized they had taken so much. And they could take everything from me except my mind and my heart. Those things I would have to give away. I decided not to give them away." President Clinton concluded, "I see here today that you have decided not to give your mind and your heart away. I ask you now to share it with all your fellow Americans."

After the president finished his remarks, the students were invited to meet him at the stage. I tried to be one of the first students to shake his hand, but by the time I reached the stage there was already a wall of people. Instead, I stood on a chair and watched as the president and Mrs. Clinton gradually made their way through the massive crowd of bodies. When they approached me I reached down and shook the president's hand. Mrs. Clinton stood a foot away, so I reached down and shook her hand as well. I was in awe; I had actually looked the president of the United States in the eye and shook his hand.

I regrouped with my friends and we discussed what we thought about the president and his speech and learned who was able to meet him. About fifteen minutes later, I looked back toward the stage and saw that the president was still shaking hands. I decided to shake his hand again. Soon enough, I was once again at the stage among throngs of people. Some kids gave him hugs and others asked him questions. I was too afraid to ask him any questions, and I didn't feel comfortable hugging him. I'd worn a fishing hat that day, and when I shook his hand again, he said, "I like your hat." I thanked him and returned to my friends.

We had to stay in the gym for an hour after President Clinton left. It had been a long day, and we all just wanted to go home; we didn't understand why we were forced to stay. Later officials told us they had been worried the students would rush the president's helicopter.

Life returned somewhat to normal, though school at Chatfield wasn't really school at all. Since our backpacks and supplies had been locked away in the vacated school lockers and classrooms, local companies had donated school supplies for our use at Chatfield. Class time was spent writing letters to the many people who poured out their condolences and prayers for us. In Mrs. Miller's chemistry class, though, she held true to her promise and her tradition of tie-dyeing T-shirts at the end of the year. It was mandatory for our teachers to give us a final, so they made us write our names down on a sheet of paper and turn it in.

To our great joy, school was let out before the end of May.

One day early in our summer vacation the police finally gave approval for students to collect backpacks and personal belongings from Columbine. Mom had taken my sister and me on a vacation to Tennessee to see Graceland (I've been an Elvis Presley fan my whole life) and to Nauvoo, Illinois, our family's favorite place to visit. We needed to get away from the chaos, media, and emotional drain we felt in Littleton. My dad couldn't miss work for the trip, so he was able to go to the high school to collect my sister's backpack. Dad said my backpack was apparently still being held, but he didn't know why. Dad reported he was not allowed to walk down certain hallways because the carpets and walls had not yet been cleaned. He said the hallways smelled acrid and empty—like death. He found my sister's backpack on the stage of the auditorium. (She was eating in the cafeteria when the shooting began, but personal belongings were later moved to the auditorium.) When the small bomb detonated, the sprinkler system soaked everything. Kathy's backpack was still wet more than a month later.

When my mom, sister, and I returned from our vacation, I was told I could go to Columbine and get my backpack. Mom came with me. Parked behind the school was a trailer filled with bags and other belongings. The school dean waited outside and marked on her list that the right people collected their belongings. I told her my gym clothes were still in the athletic locker room. She "unofficially" allowed my mom and me into the school to get my uniform.

We entered through the weight room. It was barren of the equipment and posters that usually hung from its walls. The rubber mats on the floor were also missing. I was curious to see more, so after I grabbed my tennis shoes and gym uniform, we proceeded through the school. The carpets were stripped, leaving only hard concrete floors. Mom followed me to my locker. It was eerie being in Columbine again. Almost two months before, people were running for their lives down these same hallways. Bullets screamed and bombs exploded. It had been a war zone.

We walked toward the science classroom where my sister and Coach were that day, but I couldn't make myself walk down the hall and look inside the classroom. Instead, we crossed to the staircase and around the corner to the front of the library. Along the way I saw bullet holes scattered in the aluminum window frames. The drywall had already been patched. The library entrance consisted of two large wooden doors with large windows on either side. The windows were covered in black paper and the doors were barricaded with orange crime-scene tape. When Columbine opened again for the next school year, this entrance was hidden by lockers—virtually erased as though the library had never existed. Mom and I started to walk back. As I came to an aluminum door, I placed my fingers in the bullet holes. I wanted a further sense of the reality of what had happened. Then we left as quietly as we had arrived.

In March 2000, I concluded my senior basketball season. That same month, I took a trip to England with Mrs. Samson's AP English class. An elementary school in Dunblane, Scotland, had suffered a school shooting in 1996 that left eighteen people dead. We made a point to stop in Dunblane and visit with those who had suffered. I was interested to hear what advice they would have for us, since they had also survived a school shooting. They had had four years to rebuild and heal, so I assumed they would be experts on the recovery process.

Our buses drove down the cobblestone road into town. We walked into an assembly room and were treated to punch and cookies. It was a cozy setting, but one where we could still move about and mingle. I talked with two mothers who had children in school that day and survived without physical injury. We shared our experiences and the steps we took to live a normal life again. I was still learning how to cope with the effects of Columbine, such as a friend's subsequent suicide and my own depression. I hoped desperately the people of Dunblane would have some cure-all advice or strategy to make the pain go away, but they didn't. They could only tell me that time slowly relieves the pain. It won't ever go away completely, but enough for life to continue. I knew the passing of time was not enough to erase my depression. I had to willingly make the effort to change my attitude and situation and actively turn away from being a helpless victim. I had to take control if I was going to be able to discover happiness and peace again. But I wasn't sure how. I left Dunblane feeling more upset, alone, and sad than I had been before arriving.

I had been told by medical experts and psychologists that sharing my experience, especially with others who have experienced the same kind of tragedy, would ease my heartache and pain. I followed all the advice: I talked about my feelings; I lived in an environment where I could monitor my safety and be in control of my surroundings; I sought counseling. I did just about everything short of taking prescription drugs. Yet I was still missing something. Science could tell me what the symptoms of post-traumatic stress disorder were. Science could also suggest some strategies and medications that would help me to cope with the symptoms until enough time passed for the tragedy to no longer affect me as severely. But science couldn't answer my questions.

Why did this happen? Why did people I know and love die? When will the hurt go away? How could I cope with my depression and the other unwanted changes in my life? The trauma of that day left a void in me that was rapidly filling up with feelings of guilt, anxiety, and fear. Would I ever be happy again? Logically, I knew we all have the ability to choose and that sometimes another person's choices significantly impact our lives for good or ill. But my heart couldn't deal with it. My heart didn't know *why;* my heart didn't feel peace. After the shooting I floundered around on my own looking for a peace and steadiness that eluded me. I felt abandoned and sabotaged. No one knew how I felt, nor would they ever. The worst part was that I desperately wanted to feel peace. My heart was broken and I needed it to be fixed. I didn't want to feel sad anymore.

The shootings at Columbine caused some members of our community to say there was no God, because if there was, this tragedy never would have happened. To this day I don't know why those fifteen people died so violently that day. What I do know is that the majority of our community went in search of God. Church houses filled as people sought answers. I asked the Lord why he allowed this tragedy to happen. I prayed for days and days, hoping to learn *why*. My heart was filled with confusion and doubt, and I sometimes wondered if God was even there. My prayers ached with pain and longing, yet I felt no response or comfort from him.

Then I was led by my bishop to Doctrine and Covenants 58:3–4. It reads:

> Ye cannot behold with your natural eyes, for the present time, the design of your God concerning those things which shall come hereafter, and the glory which shall follow after much tribulation.

> For after much tribulation come the blessings. Wherefore the day cometh that ye shall be crowned with much glory; the hour is not yet, but is nigh at hand.

While the scripture didn't answer my question specifically, it did give me comfort and a reason to be patient. I realized the Lord loves us and that everything happens to us for a reason and does not occur in vain. If all the answers were given to us on a silver platter without any effort on our part, it would defeat the purpose of life. Life isn't easy; life is meant for us to grow and learn from our experiences. It would be pointless if we couldn't experience both the joys and hardships of life for ourselves. It would be like playing a video game where all the hints flash before our eyes. At first the game would be fun because we couldn't lose and it would be easy to advance, but the game would soon become predictable and boring. The scripture my bishop shared with me gave me the hope and faith to keep living life and moving forward. I'm no longer resentful of my trials. Instead I look forward to the next hurdle. The Lord is in control of the earth; I can be in control of my attitude.

Sometimes people tell me, "I know I could never go through what you did." I simply reply, "You will know the kind of person you are when the chips are down." Countless people have survived events ten times worse than Columbine. Countless more will survive tragedies in the future. Yet sometimes we are able to get back up when our reason tells us it's impossible. Somehow we are able to move forward when the odds are stacked against us and our world looks hopelessly bleak. I would like to argue that we are able to do those things because we are children of God. We are entitled to God's help when we are obedient and honor our covenants. We have a purpose to our lives and tasks that only we can achieve. We have made promises to God that we will return to him. No matter the hardships we face, we will do what we said we would do and we will be who we said we would be. God didn't send us here to fail. Some of the things we are called to endure will take every last ounce of the strength we have left. But God will not leave us to endure it alone nor will he give us more than we can handle. The Lord wants to bring out the divine in all of us.

I like to think the trials I faced and my eventual recovery are like a basketball season. Conditioning workouts begin as soon as the preceding season ends in March.

Scrimmages start by mid-April. Even during summer break you work out every day, being timed in running sprints and the mile. All of your free time belongs to the coach. He pushes you until every muscle in your body hurts. You think he is out to punish you, and you think you hate him. You wonder, if basketball is supposed to be fun, why is it so hard? Some of your teammates complain and others quit. Soon the season begins, and you notice something interesting: your opponents get winded sooner than you do. The hard preseason workouts prepared you, and now you are stronger and faster; you win games. Because you grasped the basics early, the coach could work on perfecting your skills. You play ball at a level that never would have been possible without enduring those summer runs.

Life is sometimes like a basketball season. The Lord allows us to suffer because it will encourage our growth. Some people will develop new skills from their trials. Others quit when the challenges grow too demanding and they lose sight of the big picture. But for those who endure trials with faith, trust, and diligence, their final reward is that much sweeter because they know they did their best to endure the pain. They earned the reward. They won the game.

We can't always see how obstacles and hardships make us stronger. Sometimes we don't fully recognize our growth until we are farther down the road. Enduring what I never thought possible strengthened my character. I began to develop patience, compassion, and love for all people. I feel I have been able to step forward into a new dimension of maturity because of my experiences. I feel ready to continue with the next challenge of my life.

It was hard to recover from the shootings, but the ordeal forced me to truly put my trust in the Lord and allow him to take over when I could no longer function. How we endure adversity not only proves our worth to God, but, more importantly, it also proves our worth to ourselves. We are powerful people because of the inheritances we received from Heavenly Father, and we can access that power when our actions are in harmony with the Lord's teachings. He wants to make more out of us than we can see. Sometimes it takes a lifetime to understand *why* certain things happened to us, but in the meantime we can keep things in perspective and continually strive to do what is right. Trust the Lord. He loves you!

Everyone experiences dark days. The darkness comes when we feel powerless to control the injustices and sadness surrounding us. Yet we can carry on with faith and courage to step forward, to overcome our adversities, and to endure in our search for happiness. Life *is* bearable. Tomorrow *will* be a better day, depending on the attitude we choose to have. I chose happiness and have stepped into the light of a new day.

— AMBER —

A week and a half after the shootings, my brother Michael and I attended our first day at Chatfield High School. In May, I graduated from high school. I participated in some group counseling sessions through the Church, but eventually I couldn't cope with any more counselors and I stopped going. I was ready to forget about the whole thing and pretend it never happened.

Columbine still got a lot of publicity over the summer,

Amber Huntington, age 21

and I had more interviews with the police. I really wanted to just leave everything behind, so that summer I moved to Salt Lake City, Utah, to stay with my Grandma Huntington and attend the community college in the fall.

I was not sleeping at night, and I hoped that by moving away I would be able to sleep, but my insomnia followed me to Salt Lake. I dreaded nighttime; once I fell asleep I lost control of my surroundings. The smallest noise bothered me, and I would think someone was coming after me. I would sit at the window all night watching to see if anyone was coming. This time, I thought, I would see them first and have time to get away. It bothered me that I had heard gunshots in the library ten minutes before the gunmen actually came in, but I assumed it was construction. I was determined not to make that mistake again. This time I would be ready. Eventually I would fall asleep around 4:00 or 5:00 A.M. I missed a lot of my morning classes because I was so exhausted.

My heart would race at the sound or sight of police cars, ambulances, fire engines, or helicopters. I was especially sensitive to loud noises. Watching movies was torture because of the loud noises and exaggerated sound effects. Even going out in public was an ordeal. I felt anxious everywhere I went, and I would pick out people to keep an eye on in case they suddenly pulled out a gun. Sometimes I would scare myself so much I would have to leave the area.

Libraries were especially terrifying places. When I started college I would force myself to stay in the library for at least thirty minutes every day. I felt I was making progress until one scary experience during my first semester. It was the middle of September, and the college was having their yearly ceremony celebrating the start of a new school year. My first class was cancelled and I decided to spend some time in the library. I was on the main floor using the computer when I heard loud booming sounds coming from outside. I jumped up from my chair, grabbed my things, and yelled at the other kids around me, "We have to get out of here!" Some people looked at me strangely, but nobody got up. *Oh, well!* I thought. *This time I'm getting out. At least I warned them.* I ran out the door, heart pounding and adrenaline pumping, only to find the noises were from small cannons the school fired at the beginning of the ceremony in the amphitheater. I was so shaken up by the event that I didn't go back to the library for six months.

I was lost and confused. Crying, I ran all over campus looking for my friend Jess, who had been with me in the

Columbine library, and for other people from Columbine. After circling the campus a few times, I finally realized I would not be able to find them because I was the only one there from Columbine. I was the only one who was scared by the cannons. I felt so alone and alienated.

I left campus, not caring that I still had another class, and drove home. I cried so hard the road looked like a black river. It's amazing I made it home. I didn't want my grandma to see me in tears, so I stopped somewhere to compose myself. It seemed that I was going to have this deep emotional upset for the rest of my life, and I felt powerless to stop it.

Before Columbine, I would have thought someone in my situation would be fine after a couple of weeks. After all, I wasn't injured physically. What I didn't realize was that mental and emotional injuries can go even deeper. I wasn't sure what to do, so I decided to just wait it out. Maybe after a year everything would go away. But problems don't go away just because you want them to. They go away only after you spend a lot of time and energy working them away.

I enrolled in spring semester because that's what everyone else was doing. They had direction; maybe if I followed them, I would too. I didn't have many friends or talk much to anyone. I tried to get involved in the college social scene, but the friendships I started rarely lasted more than a few weeks. I felt alone and suspicious of other people. If someone asked what high school I went to, I would make something up. I had figured out that telling the truth was worse than lying. When people learned I was from Littleton, their relentless questions were too much for me to handle. What scared me more than the questions, though, was the way they looked at me afterwards.

The closer it got to April 20, the more nervous I became. I had already decided I wouldn't go to school on the one-year anniversary of the shootings because even in Salt Lake City the media was discussing Columbine on the news and in the papers. I wasn't willing to hear any mention of it in my classes. I was relieved to hear that school had been cancelled that day in Littleton. I was worried about the safety of my brother and sister who still went to the high school.

I spent the one-year anniversary with my friend Liz Carlston and her family, who were in Salt Lake City visiting relatives. Liz was still a senior at Columbine, but we had kept in touch through letters. She and I drove to Provo, Utah, to meet with some other friends from Columbine, including Gabby Harris and Mandy Nichols. No one wanted to talk much about the school; we were simply happy to be in each other's company.

When I finished my first year of college, I decided to return home for the summer. Things hadn't changed as I had hoped they would. It had been a year and I still couldn't sleep at night, and my anxiety and stress seemed to be worse than before.

I didn't want to go to a therapist or be medicated for my problems, so I continued to ignore my situation. I didn't want to deal with my feelings because that would mean I would have to accept what had happened as a real part of my life. I never wrote in a journal and never wanted to admit to being at Columbine. Yet ignoring it was hard, since the events of April 20 played in my mind every single day.

That summer, I worked as a camp counselor and found some happiness for the first time in a long time. Though Columbine was still in the papers and on the news more than I liked, it was nice to be home with my family and to attend church with my friends again. It was a relief to be able to talk to my friends again and try to work through my feelings. I felt comfortable and safe when I was with them, and I relished those feelings because they had been in such short supply over the previous year.

I moved back to Salt Lake City for fall semester and enrolled in four classes. Luckily, I found a great job at a local elementary school running the after-school program. The kids had a way of making me feel good about myself, and when I was with them I could almost forget my problems. I loved working after school every day. My job was a safe haven from my growing depression. My PTSD symptoms had stayed with me for over a year, but at least I could go to work and enjoy the happy atmosphere there.

I also found a lovely park to walk in when I wanted to be alone. I walked there often, and my thoughts always turned to Columbine. I wondered when it would finally be over for me. I didn't want to live that way anymore. I wanted to be a different person. Since junior high, I had looked forward to college where I could be a different person, where I could branch out, and where I could make new friends—including, hopefully, boyfriends. Now, here I was, a sophomore in college, feeling that I was even less like the person I wanted to be than I had been in junior high. How was I ever going to develop into the new me now, when even the simplest tasks like falling asleep at night or going to the movies were a challenge?

When I began waking up in the morning with

stomachaches, I thought maybe it was only a virus or something. But the closer I traveled to school, the worse my stomach ached. By the time I arrived on campus, I was almost too dizzy to make it to my classes. I had to stop at the library to sit down and try to regain my composure. When I did reach the classroom, my heart pounded, my stomach churned, and the room spun around me. I couldn't stay any longer, so I left. *What is wrong with me now?* I wondered.

When I returned home, the symptoms subsided and I facetiously concluded I must be allergic to school. After two weeks of the same symptoms every day, and many missed classes, I finally decided to go see the doctor. By then it was November and I only had six weeks of the semester left. I had to find a way to finish my classes.

The doctor examined me, pushing and poking, but it was not until we discussed Columbine that he knew what was wrong. He prescribed some medication to help me sleep and to start balancing out the chemicals that had built up in my body. He also gave me the names and numbers of some people to call for counseling.

It was apparent from my physical symptoms that I could not go to school. It seemed like such a waste—the books I'd bought, the homework I'd completed—but, physically and mentally, I just couldn't do it; I was too weak. I'd lost ten pounds in two weeks and most of the color in my complexion. I felt like so much had already been taken away from me—my sleep, my ability to have friends and go places—now, I couldn't even go to school. It upset me even to think about it.

I felt totally worthless as a person. I thought about the kids in the library who had been killed and wondered about them. If any of them had had the chance to live, would they have done a better job of it than I had? I thought they probably would have, and my survivor's guilt started plaguing me. Why should I have the opportunity to live instead of them? I wasn't any better than them, so why did I live? I wished once again I could switch places with any one of those fallen friends.

I had to get to the park, my haven, my special place, to think. Thoughts of worthlessness and self-hatred filled my mind. I thought of all the medications in my cupboard. I envisioned pouring out the contents of the bottles and taking all of them at once. Columbine came to me once again, and I wished that instead of hiding under my table I would have cried out or shown myself and stayed behind with the other kids. Then I remembered my prayer under the table that day. I knew the girl under the table wasn't ready to die that day. I remembered her feelings as she silently prayed to hold on to her life. Somehow I had to figure out how to keep holding on now.

Luckily, the school received a letter from my doctor and agreed to refund my tuition for that semester. What was I going to do now? At least I could still work at my job. That was really my only consolation at that point. I was going home for Christmas, and maybe my parents and I could decide then what my future plans should be. I decided to enroll for spring semester just in case I was able to solve my problems over the break.

It felt good to be back in Colorado, where I found some comfort with my friends and family. I decided to receive my patriarchal blessing while I was home from school. I remembered that many of my friends from church said they remembered the promises in their patriarchal blessing on the day of the shootings at Columbine and that was how they were able to get through it; they had the hope and knowledge they would be okay. My scheduled date arrived, and that evening my parents and I went to the patriarch's house. The blessing was a miracle; those special words were just for me. It gave me hope to hear what my Heavenly Father thought of me and to be reminded of his faith in me. After I received my blessing, I thought that somehow I was actually going to make it out of this mess.

Spring semester arrived, and I returned to Salt Lake to attend the classes I had registered for. I also made an appointment with the therapist in Salt Lake referred to me by my doctor, but I still wasn't willing to take the time to really deal with my problems, so I didn't see the counselor regularly.

I started medications for my anxiety and depression, and they seemed to help. The doctor also gave me some extra pills to take to calm me down before school. The Sunday before my first day of classes, I fasted and prayed that I would have the strength to go to class. I drove to school, and when I started to feel those symptoms come over me again, I took one pill in the car. Then while walking to my class, I took another one. I was early and the longer I waited for class to begin, the more nervous I became. Finally, the teacher came in and began to introduce the material. I was sick—feverish and dizzy—and I only lasted thirty-five minutes before I had to leave. I was so disappointed in myself, I didn't even want to try to go to my next class. I went home instead.

I stayed in my room and cried. I wondered when I would be able to go to school again and exactly how I was going to make myself do it. It wasn't like there was a switch in my head I could turn on and off. I couldn't control the panic I felt. I would just sit in class and it would happen. I began to doubt whether I *could* do anything about it at all. It wasn't just at school anymore, either. I was feeling panicked in stores, restaurants, even church. It was starting to control me, and I didn't know what to do to make it go away. All my friends were in college and moving forward with their lives, but I was moving backward, losing time.

I tried to pray for the strength to make it through one more day, but praying was hard for me. I felt a lot of survivor's guilt because Heavenly Father saved my life and I couldn't do anything with it. I didn't want to ask for help or for anything when I prayed. I figured he had already spared my life—how could I be ungrateful for that and ask for more?

I still hadn't found the right medication to help me sleep, so every day was a struggle. I tried lots of medications, but switching between them was tiring and often made me sick. It was almost a matter of deciding which side effects I could live with. My emotions were on a roller coaster, with no breaks between the huge hills. I'd go up really high, then straight down—over and over again. Finally, I found a good medication for my anxiety/depression and continued taking it. Finding one to make me fall asleep was more difficult.

I continued to work with children at a day care and running an after-school program through June because my parents were planning a trip to Utah for the Fourth of July. The Fourth of July wasn't a fun holiday for me anymore. I could handle listening to and watching the fireworks we lit because I watched us light them. It was much worse hearing loud noises from around the neighborhood and not knowing exactly what they were or who was responsible.

That summer I also took a physics class over the Internet so I could continue doing some kind of schoolwork. It made me feel a little better to be proactive about my schoolwork, and I learned a great lesson about time. I was on my own schedule, so when I was ready to work I would, and that was good enough for me.

When I returned to Colorado with my family in early July, we found out my grandma who lived in southern Colorado was in the hospital, and the doctors didn't think there was any more they could do for her. She had been sick with heart problems for more than half her life.

My mom and I left immediately for Alamosa. We met with family in the hospital and had a family prayer. Grandma was in a tremendous amount of pain, and it was time for us to let her go. Before leaving the hospital we all crowded into her room, and my uncles gave her a blessing. I cried through the entire thing, but I felt it brought a strong feeling of peace into the room.

My grandma passed away the morning of July 16, 2001. At the viewing, I found it hard to be in the same room as the casket. My mom told me the casket held just the body, that grandma's spirit was still living. Her words calmed me down, and I knew everything would be okay. She had left behind a great legacy—four children, twenty-seven grandchildren, and three great-grandchildren. My grandma's body looked very peaceful in the casket.

I was going to play the piano while my cousin played her violin as part of grandma's funeral service. Feeling panicked, I didn't know if I could make it through the funeral. I was sick and anxious, so I took some of my medication and went in the bathroom to pray. I just wanted to make it through the funeral and play the piano for my grandma so she would know I was part of the ceremony. I had to find the courage somewhere to quiet the panic just for a few hours—the panic could have the rest of my day, but I wanted these two hours for my grandma.

Once the funeral began, I felt a spirit of peace settle over me. I was determined to think only of my grandma and not to give in to my anxiety or run away. I joined my cousins on the stand to sing a song. How proud my grandma must have been at that moment when all twenty-seven of her grandchildren, plus their spouses, sang for her. After I finished singing, I knew I could make it through the service. I had received the boost I needed. I played the piano and stayed for the entire service.

Looking back, I realized I had lived one of my favorite quotes: "Courage is not the absence of fear, but the realization that something else is more important." Believing that my grandmother's funeral was more important than my fears helped me conquer my panic that day.

My mom told me about my grandma and her habit of setting goals. When my mom served a mission, my grandma's health was so bad that she set a goal to live long enough to see her return home. Her next goal was to live long enough to see my mom get married and then to see her first grandchild born. My grandma's last goal was to make it to her eightieth birthday, which she missed by only four months. My grandma was a fighter, always working to keep going, always making goal after goal.

I thought about the direction of my own life. I wasn't going anywhere because of my anxiety. After my grandmother's funeral, I made a conscious decision to fight my fears. I was going to fight for my life and my right to be happy. In the Columbine library, I couldn't fight against my attackers, so Heavenly Father stepped in to fight for me. Now, my attackers were in my mind, but I was personally able to fight this time. I knew it was going to take a lot of strength and energy, but I also knew that with Heavenly Father's help I could win.

But what did I want to do with my life? Where was I trying to go? The answer was surprisingly simple: I wanted to serve a mission. My twentieth birthday was approaching, so I had one year to get ready. After Columbine and my illness, the idea of a mission seemed out of reach—it would either have to wait or I just couldn't go—but during my grandma's funeral my dream of someday serving a mission kept coming back to me. I knew it would be tough to prepare for a mission. I would have to battle to change my mind, my thought processes, and my attitude. But now I had a goal, and I would not yield until it was accomplished. I was not going to give up on that dream that started in Primary. I couldn't give up on the little girl who was still inside me and who wrote in her first journal at age eight: "I am going to be a missionary."

I moved back to Salt Lake at the end of August and began to prepare for a mission. During church, I would try sitting closer to the front and talk myself through the anxiety I felt. At first it was hard to ignore the impulse to run away. I had to keep telling it no. Sometimes I would close my eyes and concentrate only on my breathing. I knew I was not on my own. I relied greatly on my Heavenly Father to give me the strength to fight my feelings. He never left me, and I put my total trust in him.

People are prone to mistakes, but I learned to put my total faith in my Heavenly Father and my Savior Jesus Christ. They are perfect beings, always fighting for me and what's best for me. The finest thing in my life was prayer. I had gained a powerful testimony of prayer in the library at Columbine. Prayer works, and Heavenly Father listens. I would pray all day long for Heavenly Father to keep giving me strength to conquer my fears. Of course he didn't suddenly erase my anxiety—I had to be willing to fight too—but I could feel he was by my side during my struggles.

I had to accept the fact that I might have to live with some effects of post-traumatic stress disorder for the rest of my life. Even though it had been two years since Columbine, loud noises or screams would still cause me to flash back and panic. One evening I was getting ready to go out with my friends when I heard loud, booming noises. My grandma said she didn't know what they were, but she thought they were fireworks. I grabbed the phone and locked myself in my room, shaking and crying. My heart pounded as I dialed the police. I told the officer there were loud noises in my neighborhood and I thought something bad was happening. I told her the area I lived in, and she said the local high school was having their homecoming game and setting off fireworks as part of the halftime show. I said a solemn "Thank you," and hung up. I sank to the floor feeling foolish. I was relieved but still shaky as I left late to meet my friends.

Accepting PTSD as part of my life was perhaps the best thing I could do for myself. I learned that sometimes it's better to accept our disabilities and live with them than to exhaust ourselves trying to change things we can't.

I was finally starting to feel good about my trials and myself. I was so grateful for all my blessings and for my chance to live. I stopped wishing I'd been one of the students killed in the library. I was able to accept that the tragedy at my high school was going to be a part of my life forever. I was no longer embarrassed or ashamed of being a graduate of Columbine. Columbine, for me, was now about survival and overcoming challenges placed in my way.

When one of my friends from high school, Carly Croft, moved to Salt Lake not five miles from where I lived, I knew the Lord was still watching out for me. I told her often it wasn't a coincidence, and that she had really moved there for me. We often discussed how isolated we felt because no one from our school was nearby and few people could relate to our experiences. We often discussed the incident and how to deal with it.

October 20, 2001, was special because it was the two-and-a-half-year anniversary of the shootings. My friend and I decided to have our own ceremony at a popular angel statue in the Salt Lake City Cemetery. We brought candles and one flower for each person who died at Columbine. We cried, and each of us left a letter with our feelings on the statue, along with the flowers. I felt uplifted and complete after the ceremony.

My next victory came when I had to attend an actual class in an actual classroom. I prayed and fasted and told myself that it would be okay if I still wasn't ready to go back to class, but I had to keep trying until I reached my goal. Giving up was no longer an option. I sat in the seat closest to the door. *Everything will be fine,* I told myself. *Heavenly Father is with me and he will help me.* Class started, and my stomach felt uneasy. I glanced at the clock to see how much time had passed. I had to make it through this class! The pill I had taken right before class calmed me down, and I could feel it making me numb. It was still a fight to stay in my seat for the entire hour, but I did it!

Ecstatic, I left class and ran to the library to call my mom and tell her the good news. I was so thrilled with my success that I ran and skipped out to my car. That first week was still a trial, but the days got easier and soon I didn't even have to take an extra pill in the morning. To me this meant so much more than just being able to go to school again—it meant I could serve a mission!

Throughout this whole process, I was actually starting to become the person I felt like I was inside, the person I dreamed of being in high school, the person I could feel but not touch. I was breaking through my shyness barriers. It was really happening; my dreams were coming true. I started dating during the middle of the semester and going to the Church's single adult dances with Carly and other friends. I still had problems and challenges, but now they seemed much smaller.

I was regularly taking two medications, one for anxiety and one for sleep, which had only minimal side effects. My therapist discussed with me how I might have a sleeping disorder for a long time or even the rest of my life. I just accepted this. What else could I do except accept it and not worry about it? I felt so happy. I was actually excited about my future for once. I finally felt like I had a future.

The first week in June, I visited with my bishop in Salt Lake. He often asked me to come in and chat to see how I was doing and learn if there was anything I needed. He said he had noticed a great change in me since the beginning of the year. I said, "Yeah, I know."

I left feeling amazed and pleased that he had noticed a change. As I walked home I slowly realized I had conquered it—the Columbine trials were over for me; they were finally over! I was so overwhelmed that I started to cry. I remembered all those days I thought I would never get better, that I had no future because I was too weak to deal with my problems. Now, so overcome with gratitude, I went into my backyard, knelt down, and began to pray. I could hardly speak, since I was crying and crying. I simply thanked my Heavenly Father for helping me overcome my trials and for helping me to become a better person. I thanked him for saving my life while I was under the table in the Columbine library. I told him how much I loved my life. I apologized for ever feeling like I didn't want it, because now I knew what an awesome gift life is. I prayed I would always remember my blessings and have a thankful heart. I thanked him for never leaving me alone in my struggles. I thanked him for loving me.

The next Sunday I surprised my bishop by telling him I wanted to turn in my mission papers as soon as possible. Shocked and excited he said, "Okay, let's get busy." I turned in my papers to my stake president on my birthday, August 6, 2002. I had only one more week of school left, but I would continue to work at the day care until it was time to leave. I anxiously awaited my call, the letter that would tell me where I was going to live and serve for the next eighteen months.

The letter came on September 5, 2002. My relatives and friends gathered at my uncle's house in Salt Lake City. I was on the phone with my family in Colorado as I opened my call. I screamed over the phone, "I'm going to the Dallas Texas Mission!" I couldn't believe it. I was really going on a mission, and my departure date was November 13, 2002, just two months away. "Look at me," I wanted to yell to the world. "Look at what I've done!" I wanted to tell everyone that I overcame the most trying challenge ever to face me, and I wanted them to see that they could do the same. It took me three years to overcome some major difficulties of trauma, anxiety, and depression, but I did it. I was back on track with my life. Yes, bad things happen to good people, but the Lord never leaves them alone to deal with it. There is a God and a Savior keeping watch with our best interests in mind.

Events that start out masked as tragedies usually can be turned into immense periods for growth. We need to give ourselves time to work things out, but we shouldn't be afraid to get right to the core of the problem. We must decide how we will cope with our lives—whether we are going to dwell on the tragedy or whether we will grow from it. I had a choice to make. I could live in fear of everybody and everything, or I could take a risk and live my life. A friend gave me a card that I hung on my wall. It reads in big letters, "RISK: A ship in the harbor is safe, but that's not what ships were made for."

The simplest and purest thing I know is that God truly is watching out for my best interests. He knows infinitely more than I do about everything, so he is obviously the best source to turn to. Knowing he is there is how I can sleep at night instead of sitting at the window watching for potential madmen. God knows what is best for me, and if something bad does happen to me, I know he will not leave me. That is all I need to know.

We can also draw strength from friends and family as they bless us with their encouraging words and prayers. Though I had to pull myself out of the tragedy, just knowing my friends and family were there added to my strength. (And if you have a friend or family member who has undergone a traumatic experience, be sensitive to their fears and their feelings. You don't have a perfect knowledge of what they are going through, but know that a mental illness is just as serious as a physical illness and can be just as debilitating.)

When tragedy strikes, then, it is important that we keep moving forward and not let the evil we have witnessed take up space within our souls. God will be with us. Life is a gift—we can't waste it. Our time here is short, and too many people realize that too late. Every day we live we get closer to the day we die, but it is up to us to either live each of those days or simply die. Hard times *will* come, and when they do, we can take it as a challenge to discover and improve ourselves. The ability to gain knowledge is a blessing, so we must never stop learning. And remember, there is truly no time like the present to tell the people we love how we feel.

It is often at our weakest moments that we are able to draw on inner strength we never knew we had. Because we are children of God, we have more power than we realize. It is truly amazing what we can accomplish when we use this power for good.

I cherish the message my Heavenly Father gave me in the library when I first started to pray. He let me know I would survive and live, but I had to stay there and wait. And he did not leave me: *Just be patient, endure the pain, and afterwards you will be okay. I am with you.* Heavenly Father has told us we would come to earth and would experience pain and endure terrible situations, and he won't always immediately save us from the pain. But he has promised us that we are going to be okay; we are going to make it. We have to be patient and work hard at things we would not choose on our own. We have to endure to the end. He will never leave us without comfort when we humbly and faithfully ask for it.

Work is the key on the road to our success. At the beginning of my trials, I took the lazy approach and opted to let time heal my wounds instead of working through them myself. Later I realized I would have to work hard to get what I wanted. I learned I should use my trials as stepping-stones to great things instead of carrying them like rocks on my back. We all carry around unnecessary stones—let's lighten our loads.

This world is tough, and it is only going to get tougher. We are witnesses to too many evils these days. How do we stand tall with strength to endure? The answer is found in one of my favorite scriptures, Helaman 5:12:

> And now, my sons, remember, remember that it is upon the rock of our Redeemer, who is Christ, the Son of God, that ye must build your foundation; that when the devil shall send forth his mighty winds, yea, his shafts in the whirlwind, yea, when all his hail and his mighty storm shall beat upon you, it shall have no power over you to drag you down to the gulf of misery and endless wo, because of the rock upon which ye are built, which is a sure foundation, a foundation whereon if men build they cannot fall.

I have found truth, meaning, and purpose in my life. I know what I am doing here and where I am going. I once read an article in our community newspaper in which a man stated that the Columbine tragedy proves God does not exist. I disagree. I can testify that the events at Columbine are proof that God *does* exist. My life now is proof God exists. There is no doubt in my mind about it. To him and my Savior, Jesus Christ, I am eternally grateful for their never-ending love and faith in me. My life is theirs, and I hope I will always act accordingly, to do all I can to help those around me.

I am not sorry I was at Columbine on that fateful day, although I am deeply sorry for the things that occurred there. I know that the answers to my questions about the day may have to wait until I leave this earth; however, I do have all the answers I need for the present. Those answers include these truths: In order to know love, we must also know hate; in order to know happiness, we must also know sorrow; in order to know peace, we must also know war; and in order to know life, we must also know death. We must have the courage to let go of those things that bring us down. We must embrace truth, embrace goodness, embrace love—and once we have hold of these things, never let them go.

AFTERWORD

My first semester of school at Brigham Young University, I enrolled in a political science seminar that featured speakers who played key roles in significant historical events. One speaker was a 1960s civil rights activist and friend of Martin Luther King Jr., and another was an advisor to Yasser Arafat during an early 1990s Israeli-Palestinian conflict. The one I remember the best was Rick Nye, a soldier during the Vietnam War. He didn't recount all the horrid scenes he witnessed, but it was enough for me to feel as though I was one of the few in the room who could relate to how he felt and reacted. One student asked him, "How did you deal with the trauma of the war?" Mr. Nye said it was extremely difficult. He faced years of depression after the war and was haunted by flashbacks of the appalling scenes he'd witnessed. His hope and belief in God's love for him was a sustaining force. He said one helpful remedy for him was to write all his thoughts down in a journal. Once they were trapped

121

between the bindings of a book, the mental images of his past could no longer haunt or hurt him.

I took his words to heart. The murdering in 1999 at Columbine High School was an event so exploited by the media it remains in the consciousness of people even to this day. Sometimes when I wear a Columbine sweatshirt around campus people will ask me, "Are you from Columbine, Colorado?" To this I smile and can honestly answer, "No." But for those people who know Columbine is a high school and not a city, I feel pressured to answer their questions.

The questions are uniformly similar: "Were you there that day? Where were you? Did you know the kids who were involved?" After answering the very same questions for so long, I feel my answers have become scripted, void of all meaning.

I was scared to meet new people because I knew as soon as they learned where I was from, they would ask me about Columbine, thrilled to meet someone who was connected to something so enormous. But when they asked their questions, terrible memories from that April 20 would fill my head. When such conversations ended, I was left alone with those awful memories. What troubled me most was that most people only wanted to know the gory details. I wondered why they cared so much about what I'd *seen,* but not how I *felt* or what I learned.

I decided to move forward with this book for much the same reasons Mr. Nye wrote in his journals. For closure. I asked some of my friends who were also at school that day to share their stories, or to allow their stories to be told, in hopes that it would help their healing and also to pass on what they have learned to any who might be suffering.

Writing this book has been a therapeutic tool, a chance to reflect on the sinister events we endured and to create meaning from our experiences. Scattered thoughts of depression and death from Columbine no longer circle in my head, but instead are bound to the pages of journals and this work.

I hope this book is a source of understanding and inspiration for those who read it. Once word of the shooting broke out across the nation, thousands of people called radio talk shows, wrote books, articles, and even television shows all screaming out their opinions, trying to analyze the signs and the steps that should have been taken by police and school administrators to prevent the shooting. Their facts were often inaccurate, to say the least. They had it wrong, mainly because they weren't there. They could only speculate about the problems and solutions.

The truth is that the problem is us. We are too neglectful of each other, and we are selfish because it's easy. But just because something is easy doesn't make it right. I grew tired of turning on the evening news only to watch a classmate reduce their story to the level of sensationalism for their fifteen minutes of fame. Students who had something worthwhile to say often kept it to themselves because they saw how other's words and stories were altered to fit the media's agenda. The sensation-seekers always described Columbine on a superficial level, so today its name has a somber and negative connotation. The media bypassed the good that occurred in the time following the shootings.

No one expected a school shooting to happen in our quiet community. The tragedy was new territory we had to stumble our way through together. We were able to keep both our perspective and our sanity by finding whatever good in this world we could. The worst thing that would happen from the events at Columbine is if the victims died in vain. If we never learn anything from their deaths, then they did perish worthlessly. Meaning *can* be found from this tragedy when we understand ourselves and God and learn how to improve our relationships and interactions with him and each other. We should chose to take the high road, not for the admiration of other people but for the fulfillment of our souls and for the good we may do for others. When we do, we will have learned one of the greatest lessons of life.

ABOUT THE AUTHORS

Liz Carlston completed her fourth year on the varsity basketball team in March 2000 and graduated from Columbine in May 2000. In basketball she earned all-state honors and team MVP. Liz is currently serving a Spanish-speaking mission for The Church of Jesus Christ of Latter-day Saints at the Oakland California Temple Visitors' Center. When she returns in early 2005, she will complete a public relations degree at Brigham Young University. Ultimately, she hopes to work in Nashville, Tennessee, as a publicist for a country music artist or in a management position at a record company.

Amber Huntington graduated from Columbine in May 1999 and moved to Utah to attend Salt Lake Community College. She worked in a day-care center because of her love for children. In her spare time, she began learning to play the violin. Since November 2002, she has been serving as a missionary in Dallas, Texas, for The Church of Jesus Christ of Latter-day Saints. Amber will return home in July 2004.

Michael Johnson eventually recovered from the injuries he sustained at Columbine—at least enough to resume a normal life. But like many of those who were wounded, he will face some physical problems for the rest of his life. For his birthday in May 2000, Mike met with three of the seventeen people whose donated blood helped save his life. He graduated from Columbine in 2001. During his junior and senior years of high school, he worked part time to earn money for his mission. He was honorably released from serving in the California Santa Rosa Mission in June 2003.

Kathy Johnson grew up in Littleton, Colorado. She met her husband, Gary, in Utah after she attended Ricks College in Rexburg, Idaho. She is the mother of three children: Michael, Kimberly, and Stephanie. In her spare time she enjoys sewing and loves watching her children grow up.